A Treatment Manual for Justice Involved Persons with Mental Illness

A Treatment Manual for Justice Involved Persons with Mental Illness comprises a comprehensive and structured treatment manual that provides clinicians with a guide for treating justice involved persons with mental illness. The manual includes a treatment plan for each session with specific structured exercises (for both in-group and out-of-group work) designed to reach objectives. The program incorporates a psychosocial rehabilitation model, social learning paradigm and cognitive-behavioral model for change, and the cognitive-behavioral approach is evident throughout the manual. CLCO includes a companion workbook with participant handouts, worksheet and homework assignments which can be found at www.routledge.com/9781138700086

Robert D. Morgan is the John G. Skelton Jr. Regents Endowed Professor in Psychology, Chairperson for the Department of Psychological Sciences, and directs the Institute for Forensic Science at Texas Tech University. Dr. Morgan's research and scholarly activities include treatment and assessment of justice involved persons with mental illness, forensic mental health assessment, and professional development and training issues.

Daryl G. Kroner is a professor in the Criminology and Criminal Justice Department at Southern Illinois University. His primary research areas include violence risk assessment, criminal attributions, and crime desistance.

Jeremy F. Mills worked for 15 years as a psychologist within a number of federal correctional institutions and is currently a Regional Director Health Services with Correctional Services Canada. Dr. Mills is also an Adjunct Research Professor at Carleton University. His primary areas of scientific inquiry include violence risk assessment, antisocial attitudes, and the perception of violence risk.

International Perspectives on Forensic Mental Health
A Routledge Book Series

Edited by Ronald Roesch and Stephen Hart,
Simon Fraser University

The goal of this series is to improve the quality of health care services in forensic settings by providing a forum for discussing issues related to policy, administration, clinical practice, and research. The series will cover topics such as mental health law; the organization and administration of forensic services for people with mental disorder; the development, implementation and evaluation of treatment programs for mental disorder in civil and criminal justice settings; the assessment and management of violence risk, including risk for sexual violence and family violence; and staff selection, training, and development in forensic systems. The book series will consider proposals for both monographs and edited works on these and similar topics, with special consideration given to proposals that promote best practice and are relevant to international audiences.

Published Titles

Case Studies in Sexual Deviance
Toward Evidence Based Practice
Edited by William T. O'Donohue

Forensic Psychological Assessment in Practice
Case Studies
Corine De Ruiter & Nancy Kaser-Boyd

Sexual Predators
Society, Risk and the Law
Robert A. Prentky, Howard E. Barbaree & Eric S. Janus

Forthcoming Titles

Handbook of Forensic Social Work With Children
Edited by Viola Vaughan-Eden

A Treatment Manual for Justice Involved Persons with Mental Illness

Changing Lives and Changing Outcomes

Robert D. Morgan, Daryl G. Kroner, and Jeremy F. Mills

Routledge
Taylor & Francis Group

NEW YORK AND LONDON

First published 2018
by Routledge
711 Third Avenue, New York, NY 10017

and by Routledge
2 Park Square, Milton Park, Abingdon, Oxon, OX14 4RN

Routledge is an imprint of the Taylor & Francis Group, an informa business

Library of Congress Cataloging-in-Publication Data
A catalog record for this book has been requested

ISBN: 978-1-138-70007-9 (hbk)
ISBN: 978-1-138-70008-6 (pbk)
ISBN: 978-1-315-20499-4 (ebk)

Typeset in Sabon
by Apex CoVantage, LLC

Visit the eResources www.routledge.com/9781138700086

Contents

15 Module III: Thoughts and Attitudes   77

16 Module IV: Medication Adherence   98

17 Module V: Coping With Mental Illness and Criminalness   106

18 Module VI: Emotions Management   118

19 Module VII: Associates   130

20 Module VIII: Community Skills Development   148

21 Module IX: Substance Abuse   167

    References   180
    Index   183

Foreword

The International Association of Forensic Mental Health Services (IAFMHS) is an interdisciplinary professional society representing forensic professionals engaged in research and practice in forensic mental health. Its membership includes psychologists, psychiatrists, social workers, nurses, and lawyers representing over 22 countries worldwide. Its goals are to promote education, training, and research in forensic mental health and to enhance the standards of forensic mental health services in the international community. IAFMHS holds an annual conference, publishes a journal (*International Journal of Forensic Mental Health*) and a book series (International Perspectives on Forensic Mental Health).

The goal of the book series is to improve the quality of health care services in forensic settings by providing a forum for discussing issues related to policy, administration, clinical practice, and research. The series covers topics such as mental health law; the organization and administration of forensic services for people with mental disorder; the development, implementation and evaluation of treatment programs for mental disorder in civil and criminal justice settings; the assessment and management of violence risk, including risk for sexual violence and family violence; and staff selection, training, and development in forensic mental health systems.

The latest entry in the series is *A Treatment Manual for Justice Involved Persons with Mental Illness: Changing Lives and Changing Outcomes* by Robert D. Morgan, Daryl G. Kroner, and Jeremy F. Mills. I am particularly pleased to include this book in the series as it is the first one to focus solely on treatment. We have had a number of books target forensic assessment issues and some that have addressed treatment as part of a risk management strategy, but this is the first treatment manual in the series. The authors bring a vast amount of research and clinical experience to the task of creating a treatment program that can be used to change the lives of individuals who come into the justice system with serious mental health issues. As those in the field know fully well, this is a population that is increasing in both jails and prisons, and validated treatment programs are essential to address their needs and ultimately impact their lives.

The program they created is designed for use in many different settings, including jails and prisons, probation and parole services, but also forensic hospitals as well as inpatient and outpatient community mental health centers. Grounded in the Risk-Need-Responsivity treatment model and the psychosocial rehabilitation literature, it draws heavily on the group psychotherapy work of Dr. Irvin Yalom. The authors recognize that by the time individuals with serious mental health issues are arrested, the problems they face are long-standing and not susceptible to change in a brief period. They are also aware that many of these offenders have co-occurring disorders of mental illness and substance abuse, and that lasting change requires more than just a brief intervention. As a consequence, the program entails nine treatment modules that are delivered over 76 sessions to treat co-occurring disorders. Given that the program relies on a psychotherapy approach, the authors stress that service providers should be mental health professionals with formal education and training in the provision of psychotherapy. They recommend that treatment sessions should occur three times a week, with each session lasting about 1 hr 50 min. The manual lays out a detailed plan for each session. The authors have prepared an accompanying workbook that provides handouts, worksheets, and homework assignments for each session. Consistent with best practices, the structured learning exercises suggested for the sessions are based on the cognitive-behavioral and social-learning paradigms.

This manual will be of interest to a range of mental health professionals, including psychologists, social workers, correctional case managers, and others responsible for delivering treatment services in correctional and mental health settings. While Morgan and his colleagues provide some initial data to suggest it is an effective program, they clearly want to encourage ongoing research by programs implementing the model so that they can add to the body of knowledge about its effectiveness. An important feature of the manual is that each of the nine treatment modules targets a specific problem or concern, and includes pre-post testing sessions for the administration of outcome data, and a content examination. The data this will generate will provide valuable feedback on the impact of this intervention as it is implemented in diverse settings.

Ron Roesch
International Perspectives on Forensic
Mental Health Series Editor

Acknowledgments

We are indebted to the treatment providers who facilitated treatment groups, which allowed for evaluating the program. These include Drs. Rebecca Bauer, Marshall Bewley, Leah Power, and Michael Shields, and Ms. Catherine Serna. Thank you also to Stephanie Van Horn for her work on revising and improving the modular quizzes used throughout this program. Special thanks to Leah Power, Brieann McDaniel, and Sydnee Erickson for tirelessly helping with formatting and organizing the program and participant workbook. We also thank the agencies that adopted our program for use with their correctional population and provided us information on outcomes to evaluate the program (Lubbock County Community Corrections Department, Harris County Probation), as well as agencies that field tested the program and provided important fidelity data (Maine Department of Corrections, Forensic and Mental Health Services, Inc., Hamilton, Ohio). We are also very grateful to Dr. Nancy Wolff and the Center for Behavioral Health Services and Criminal Justice Research (Rutgers University) for funding a pilot of this program.

Most importantly, we are grateful to the thousands of inmates and CJ-PMI that allowed us to work with them. Working with you led to the development of the model and strategies that guide this intervention. Without you there would be no program. We thank you and we wish you much success in changing your lives and obtaining your goals.

About the Authors

Robert D. Morgan, Ph.D. completed his Ph.D. in counseling psychology at Oklahoma State University and a postdoctoral fellowship in forensic psychology in the Department of Psychiatry at the University of Missouri–Kansas City and the Missouri Department of Mental Health. He is currently the John G. Skelton Jr. Regents Endowed Professor in Psychology, Chairperson for the Department of Psychological Sciences, and directs the Institute for Forensic Science at Texas Tech University. Dr. Morgan's research and scholarly activities include treatment and assessment of justice involved persons with mental illness, effects of incarceration including in restricted housing units, and forensic mental health assessment. His research has been funded by the National Institute of Mental Health, the National Institute of Justice, and the Center for Behavioral Health Services & Criminal Justice Research. He has authored or co-authored over 80 peer-reviewed articles and book chapters, and two books: *A Clinician's Guide to Violence Risk Assessment* and *Careers in Psychology: Opportunities in a Changing World* (3rd edition). He has provided forensic mental health services at the request of courts, defense, and prosecution, and consults with state and private correctional agencies to inform practice.

Daryl G. Kroner, Ph.D. completed his Ph.D. at Carleton University, Ottawa, Canada. He is Professor in the Criminology and Criminal Justice Department at Southern Illinois University. He has published over 70 peer-reviewed papers and one book (*A Clinician's Guide to Violence Risk Assessment*), covering a variety of topics related to offender psychological and risk assessment. His primary research areas include violence risk assessment, criminal attributions, and crime desistance. He has been involved in large-scale correctional evaluations in Canada and the United States. He has served on the Executive of the Criminal Justice Section of the Canadian Psychological Association both as the co-editor of their newsletter and as chair of the section. His accomplishments have been recognized in his appointment as Fellow of the Canadian Psychological Association.

Jeremy F. Mills, Ph.D. completed his Ph.D. at Carleton University, Ottawa, Canada. He worked for 15 years as a psychologist within a number of federal correctional institutions and is currently Regional Director Health Services with Correctional Services Canada in addition to a private practice in forensic and counseling psychology. Dr. Mills is Adjunct Research Professor at Carleton University where he supervises both undergraduate and graduate students. He has served on the Executive of the Criminal Justice Section of the Canadian Psychological Association in the capacity of co-editor, editor, and chair of the section. Dr. Mills was also the chair of the first, second and third North American Correctional and Criminal Justice Psychology Conferences held in Canada. He has published over 40 peer-reviewed papers and one book (*A Clinician's Guide to Violence Risk Assessment*), covering a variety of topics related to offender assessment. His primary areas of scientific inquiry include violence risk assessment, antisocial attitudes, and the perception of violence risk. He has developed a depression-hopelessness-suicide screening instrument that has been incorporated into a nationally administered mental health screening for all offenders entering the Correctional Service of Canada. Dr. Mills is a co-investigator of research funded by the National Institute of Justice. Among other recognitions he is the recipient of the Public Service Award of Excellence for Scientific Contribution.

Program Introduction

Changing Lives and Changing Outcomes (CLCO) is intended to be a comprehensive and structured guide for your work with the criminal justice involved persons with mental illness (CJ-PMI) in your agency. The manual includes a treatment plan for each session with specific structured exercises (for both in-group and out of group work) designed to reinforce the learning objectives of each session. A workbook accompanies this treatment manual and each participant should be provided a copy of the workbook (or pages of the workbook can be distributed in conjunction with the treatment program such that pages for each session are distributed during that session). *CLCO* was developed for implementation individually or in a group setting, and is relevant for working with CJ-PMI in correctional, forensic, and community mental health settings.

This treatment manual is intended to provide you, the therapist, with a guide for treating CJ-PMI. *CLCO* can be provided to your clients regardless of their setting (e.g., probation, jail, prison, state forensic hospital, inpatient or outpatient community mental facility). *CLCO* consists of nine treatment modules delivered over 76 sessions. The treatment modules include: (1) Preparing for Change, (2) Mental Illness and Criminalness Awareness, (3) Thoughts and Attitudes, (4) Medication Adherence, (5) Coping With Mental Illness and Criminalness, (6) Emotions Management, (7) Associates, (8) Community Skills Development, and (9) Substance Abuse. The first module integrates practices of Motivational Interviewing to prepare CJ-PMI to change. The remaining modules were developed and modified from the Risk-Need-Responsivity and psychosocial rehabilitation literatures, and integrate the principles and practices of Illness Management and Recovery with best practices from the correctional rehabilitation literature. The uniqueness of *CLCO* is in the integration of best mental health practices and best correctional rehabilitation practices in each and every module. Thus, for example, the awareness module is not limited to mental illness awareness, rather, it also incorporates awareness of one's criminalness.

CLCO provides a framework for intervening when mental illness and criminality co-occur. This is keeping with recent advances in the treatment of co-occurring disorders that recommend unified treatment protocols, or a combined/interdisciplinary approach. The goal of *CLCO* is to enhance quality of life, reflected through improved mental health status and reduced criminal and psychiatric recidivism.

CLCO incorporates a psychosocial rehabilitation model, social learning paradigm, and cognitive-behavioral model for change and is consistent with a best practices model in corrections and mental health treatment. Although this treatment program utilizes a psychoeducational process, this is not a psychoeducational treatment program. Rather, *CLCO* integrates psychoeducation with a psychotherapeutic approach, specifically an interpersonal process-oriented group psychotherapy approach. As psychotherapy provides the foundation for this intervention, we review and describe an interpersonal-process oriented approach to group psychotherapy. Consistent with best correctional practices, structured learning exercises based on a cognitive-behavioral theoretical approach supplements the process-oriented work in each session. Thus, we begin with a review of psychotherapy with justice involved individuals before providing the *CLCO* treatment program (detailed module and session information). It should be noted that this manual is written in a clear and reader friendly format, thus scientific references will be implemented only as specifically warranted.

1 Evidence Base for Changing Lives and Changing Outcomes (CLCO)

CLCO has been delivered in the Lubbock County Court Residential Treatment Center (CRTC) and Lubbock-Crosby County Adult Supervision and Probation, Harris County (Texas) probation department, Maine Department of Corrections, CorrectCare services, and the Forensic and Mental Health Services, Inc., Hamilton Ohio, Butler County. Data was obtained from the Lubbock and Harris county sites for preliminary investigation of the effectiveness of *CLCO*.

Preliminary examination of *CLCO* has produced promising results. For example, in a sample of 47 CJ-PMI in a residential treatment facility, results showed evidence of strong therapeutic alliance and treatment program satisfaction, as well as reliable reductions in psychiatric symptoms and criminal thinking (see Morgan, Kroner, Mills, Bauer, & Serna, 2014). Importantly, CJ-PMI participants of *CLCO* also learned the content and principles taught to them during the various therapeutic modules (Van Horn et al., 2017). That is, participants in *CLCO* demonstrated increased knowledge acquisition as assessed from pre-module to post-module content tests. Finally, CJ-PMI who successfully completed *CLCO* were over two times as likely to successfully meet the conditions of their probation compared to CJ-PMI who were unsuccessfully discharged from the *CLCO* program (Morgan, Van Horn, & Hunter, 2017). CJ-PMI who successfully completed *CLCO* also had significantly fewer positive drug screenings ($M = 0.66$, $SD = 1.26$) than did those who did not complete (i.e., premature termination) the program ($M = 1.36$, $SD = 2.10$), $t(110.39) = -2.30$, $p = .02$, $d = .40$). Furthermore, CJ-PMI who completed the treatment program evidenced a 71% decrease in the rate of positive drug screenings before and after treatment. No significant decrease was noted among CJ-PMI who were discharged from the program.

2 Service Provider Qualifications

Service providers should be mental health professionals with formal education and training in the provision of psychotherapy. Although non–mental health professionals (e.g., paraprofessionals, criminal justice counselors) will understand the concepts and treatment strategies of *CLCO*, they will not have the prerequisite psychotherapy skills to effectively implement this program. Although *CLCO* utilizes a psychoeducational process, it is a psychotherapy program. Psychoeducation is implemented to teach CJ-PMI concepts and skills they need in order to make life changes; however, psychotherapy is necessary to help clients transfer the information they learn and skills they develop into a lifestyle change. That is, psychotherapy is necessary for long-term change to occur; thus, we consider psychotherapy training at the masters or doctoral degree to be the prerequisite level of training for service providers to facilitate *CLCO*.

3 CJ-PMI Life Goals

How do CJ-PMI change? With new prosocial life goals. Prosocial goals and behavior are defined in *CLCO* as mental illness management with active participation in relapse prevention as well as desistence from crime.

Criminal justice–involved individuals must develop personal goals that are long-term and productive. Each CJ-PMI must have personally meaningful goals for which to strive. Without long-term goals, CJ-PMI have minimal reasons to avoid behaviors that are reinforcing in the short-term, but unproductive with regard to long-term goal accomplishment (i.e., change). For example, CJ-PMI will frequently state their desire to discontinue their psychotropic treatment regimen with complaints of the negative side effects of their medications (an unfortunate reality of coping with mental illness) or the immediate gains of crime. In order to refrain from these counterproductive, yet immediately gratifying behaviors, CJ-PMI must have higher order goals that they are striving toward. Without such goals, you, as the therapist, are impotent to facilitate prosocial behavior.

This process of goal setting begins in the initial module, "Preparing for Change," and is reinforced in each therapeutic module (i.e., each of the nine treatment modules begins with a review of the CJ-PMI's productive life goals). It is your responsibility, as the therapist, to tie the principles of change and module content to each CJ-PMI's long-term goals. As noted by a doctoral student of the first author, this is particularly important because "they appreciated me remembering what they were working towards", and it helped maintain the therapeutic alliance. This is easily accomplished by highlighting CJ-PMI statements and behaviors that are supportive of change and movement toward their overarching goals, and challenges to those statements and behaviors that are counterproductive (sabotage) their work toward their goals.

A note of caution when helping CJ-PMI develop their personal goals is warranted. It is important to help CJ-PMI develop personally meaningful goals that are *realistic*. They will not benefit by developing unrealistic or overly ambitious goals, as they will lose sight of these goals during the treatment program. The simpler, more concrete, and realistic the treatment participants' goals are, the more likely they are to remain meaningful throughout the treatment program thereby providing a source of motivation.

Examples of good goals include:

- I will remain crime-free and out of correctional institutions for two years post-release (as an initial marker).
- I will obtain a job within 30 days of my release and maintain full-time employment at this job for one calendar year.
- I will have no instances of *involuntary* hospitalization in the first year that I am back in the community.
- I will miss no more than two required probation appointments in the first 6 months of probation, and I will notify my probation officer in advance every time I am going to miss an appointment.

Examples of less productive goals that are overly ambitious or not specific include:

- I will never go back to jail (or prison).
- I will never go to the hospital again.
- I am going to go to medical school and be a doctor to help people like me.

The first two examples of these less productive goals lack specificity and are life-encompassing (life-encompassing goals are by nature more difficult to achieve and remain committed to). Even in the best of circumstances, CJ-PMI may require a brief stay in a psychiatric hospital. In fact, many consider a brief voluntary admission for purposes of psychiatric stabilization to be indicative of recovery and healthy behavior. Thus, a goal that recognizes voluntary brief periods of hospitalization, but aims to eliminate involuntary hospitalization, is appropriate.

In the case of the third less productive goal, goals must be weighed in light of the individual's circumstances. Although it is certainly possible that some CJ-PMI can achieve professional goals such as advanced academic achievement or prestigious managerial positions, when stated by a 24-year-old high school dropout it is likely to be overly ambitious and not consistent with the individual's preparation or capabilities. How then to help participants achieve realistic goals without demoralizing them or breaking hope? First, it is important to instill hope in the client— hope that they can have the life they want—and then help them explore the steps necessary to achieve those goals. By breaking down their life goals into manageable (and measureable) goals, you can help your clients develop goals that are simplistic, realistic, and yet meaningful.

4   Responsibility and Criminalness

CJ-PMI are responsible for avoiding crime and managing their illness. Specifically, they must assume responsibility for achieving their long-term life goals. The principles of *Changing Lives and Changing Outcomes* are designed to facilitate increased responsibility for prosocial and productive behavior. In spite of claims to the contrary, including some scientifically proposed claims, CJ-PMI are responsible for their place in life and how well they cope with their illnesses. This is not to say that barriers do not exist or to deny that CJ-PMI are often reared in environments unfavorable toward prosocial behaviors; however, it is ultimately the individual who must accept responsibility for their situation in life.

Thus, to succeed in this program, CJ-PMI will need to accept responsibility for managing their illness and for avoiding crime: without excuses, blaming, or diversions by pointing blame at external situations or people. It is not the psychiatrists', psychologists', social workers', psychiatric nurses', or other service providers' responsibility to make the CJ-PMI well. Likewise, it is not the CJ-PMI's family or partner's fault, law enforcement officer's (including probation and parole officers) fault, or treatment provider's fault that CJ-PMI are in the justice system or engaged in antisocial acts. Responsibility lies with the individual, and an overarching principle of this program is that CJ-PMI must accept responsibility for their behaviors in all facets of their lives. This includes accepting responsibility for behaviors that appear unrelated to illness management or crime (e.g., work functioning, effectively dealing with common and everyday problems and social interactions).

It cannot be overemphasized and should be a focus of your work with any CJ-PMI: *lack of responsibility in one area is symptomatic of continued endorsement of irresponsibility in all areas.* As examples, not completing homework assignments on time, performing poorly at assigned work, and not maintaining a clean housing environment are all symptoms of an ongoing endorsement of a nonproductive lifestyle. This lifestyle is counterproductive with regard to CJ-PMI's life goals. To summarize, one goal of this program is to facilitate CJ-PMI accepting responsibility for all areas of their life, not limited to illness management and avoiding crime. Behaviors such as these, and efforts or behaviors that avoid responsibility, are examples of criminalness and should be labeled as such. It should be noted that we use the term "criminalness" here as it was developed as a useful verbal tool for helping CJ-PMI quickly and efficiently refer to their antisocial and/or offending behavior. In *Changing Lives and Changing Outcomes* we define criminalness as behavior that breaks laws and social conventions and/or violates the rights and well-being of others. This may or may not lead to arrestable offenses such as abuse of sick leave, taking office supplies for out-of-office use, drug possession, property crime, and/or person and violent crimes.

It is worth noting that criminalness is not the same as criminogenic risk. Criminalness is defined as behavior that is antisocial, non-productive by avoiding responsibility, and violates the rights and well-being of others. Such behavior may or may not lead to arrestable offenses. Criminalness is a trait that can vary in degree over time, can present in numerous ways (e.g., burglary or abusing sick leave), and can be found to varying degrees in all members of society.

We recognize that criminalness will likely be viewed as pejorative by your clients, and it promotes labeling, which is particularly problematic due to prevalent stigma encountered by both PMI and criminal justice-involved populations; however, it provides a useful strategy for discussing all behaviors (legal or illegal) that promote or contribute to antisocial behaviors or a criminal lifestyle. Furthermore, for therapeutic purposes, criminalness is easily understood by a range of criminal justice involved individuals and is commonly accepted into their everyday vocabulary (as evidenced by field testing of this intervention). Also, it provides a mechanism for CJ-PMI to evaluate their behavior.

In addition, current constructs that label CJ involved individuals (i.e., antisocial personality disorder [ASPD], psychopathy) do not contribute to the treatment of these individuals. Criminalness is a construct that bridges this gap by offering a treatment target. Furthermore, criminalness is differentiated from ASPD and psychopathy because of the emphasis on irresponsible behavior that prevents the individual from achieving prosocial, productive, and satisfying life goals—it is behavior and not a diagnosis. The necessity of goals in the treatment of CJ-PMI is tied to the concept of recovery in the psychiatric rehabilitation literature and motivational interviewing with CJ involved individuals. Recovery in the psychiatric rehabilitation literature does not refer to remission of one's mental illness, rather it refers to a return to pre-illness levels of independence and prosocial functioning with significant improvements in quality of life (Corrigan, Mueser, Bond, Drake, & Solomon, 2008). Recovery also refers to PMI's ability to control and manage their symptoms while overcoming deficits resulting from mental illness (Corrigan, 2003). Criminalness hinders the

CJ-PMI's ability to achieve recovery as it prevents the development of productive and satisfying life goals as well as the behaviors necessary to achieve such goals.

Perhaps more importantly, criminalness is generalizable to the mental health treatment of PMI. It is theorized that many setbacks in the treatment of PMI (e.g., medication noncompliance, poor attendance of mandated psychotherapy, failure to utilize social resources as discussed in treatment planning) are acts of criminalness. Therefore, the authors believe that criminalness will give clinicians added utility in explaining, defining, and predicting rehabilitation success in CJ-PMI, as well as in general psychiatric populations. This has a superior utility in the treatment of CJ-PMI, because one construct can predict success of treatments and potential roadblocks to the completion of that treatment.

Examples of criminalness from our work with CJ-PMI abound; however, one case example exemplifies the impact of criminalness on psychiatric and criminal outcomes. John was a resident in a secure treatment facility participating in our treatment program. John was diagnosed with bipolar disorder and was incarcerated for theft and drug possession. While participating in the group, John discussed a desire to remain free from the criminal justice system, but also conflicting desires to maintain a lifestyle of living in the fast lane and self-medicating his mental illness. He expressed the sentiment that illicit substances better soothed his symptoms without the negative side effects of psychotropic medications. During a recent pass from the facility, John and other members of the treatment group were eating at a fast food restaurant, but were prohibited from ordering a fountain beverage (i.e., they ordered water). John was provided a water cup and took advantage of the opportunity to fill his cup with Sprite rather than water (note: this behavior was labeled as criminalness by the other members of John's treatment group and became a point of emphasis in John's treatment and part of the larger therapeutic process). Criminalness was pervasive in John's behaviors and opposed to productive, prosocial, satisfying life goals of maintaining his freedom. Criminalness was also evidenced in John's case in his desire to self-medicate his symptoms rather than follow his prescribed treatment regimen, and in his desire to maintain a fast and carefree lifestyle regardless of the risk it placed him in for further criminal justice involvement. Furthermore, his behaviors were criminal in that he continued a pattern of theft when he encountered an opportunity to do so. To provide John mental health treatment specifically targeting issues of mental illness or criminal justice–oriented interventions targeting his criminal behavior misses the totality of John's situation. John was both mentally ill and a criminal, and he evidenced a pattern of irresponsible behavior that violates the rights and well-being of others and prevents the individual from obtaining productive, prosocial, and satisfying life goals.

Because it is central to the effectiveness of treating offending behavior in this treatment program, we conclude by restating a mantra that should be embedded in your therapeutic mindset: it cannot be overemphasized and should be a focus of your work with any individual involved in the CJ system—*lack of responsibility in one area is symptomatic of continued endorsement of irresponsibility in all areas.*

Program Goals

The primary goal of *Changing Lives and Changing Outcomes* is recovery. Recovery does not refer to recovery (or remission) of one's mental illness or criminalness. In other words, recovery for our purposes does not mean the absence of mental illness or desire for crime; rather, recovery refers to a prosocial functioning at pre-illness levels and by desistence. Successful recovery will result in significant improvements in quality of life, as CJ-PMI have increased good days, fewer hospital days and avoidance of reincarceration (based on our experience with this treatment program, your clients will appreciate your discussion of "increased good days, fewer hospital days, and staying out of jail/prison" as your goals for them). These are simple, clear, and realistic goals for you to have for your clients, and they will likely agree with the goals and appreciate the simplicity with which these are presented.

CJ-PMI are responsible for their recovery—in fact, CJ-PMI are solely responsible for their recovery. Services are in place to assist CJ-PMI's efforts toward recovery, but CJ-PMI must accept the responsibility for their own recovery. They must ask for help when help is needed. They must take the steps to control and manage their symptoms while overcoming deficits resulting from mental illness, and assume responsibility for developing goals, motivation, and skills for resisting crime.

Recovery is distinguished from cure by the emphasis on the individual's responsibility to the recovery process (identifying and pursuing personal goals). We avoid focus on a return to "normal" or "healthy" mental health functioning or the concept of offender rehabilitation (it has commonly been stated you "can't rehabilitate an offender that was never habilitated to begin with"). Recovery is both a personal as well as systemic process. Specifically, for recovery to occur CJ-PMI must accept the need for change and assume responsibility for change. We refer to this as an "internal" process because recovery necessitates CJ-PMI action. That is, for recovery to occur, CJ-PMI must develop hope and believe that recovery is possible, develop a realistic sense of self (note we are not referring to self-esteem), develop a sense of empowerment by accepting responsibility for their recovery, and connect to the prosocial world.

Although internal conditions are necessary, they are not sufficient for recovery to occur—CJ-PMI require assistance for the process of recovery to occur. Specifically, CJ-PMI need external supports (conditions) including a human rights agenda to reduce the dual stigma of mental illness and offender (convict, inmate, etc.). For recovery to occur, CJ-PMI also require a positive and safe culture to allow for healing; a culture embodied by warmth, supportive of tolerance, respect, trust, compassion, and empathy. However, this culture must also be non-tolerant of rules violations and offending behavior. Parole and probation officers need to remain supportive of CJ-PMI recovery efforts, yet also enforce rule-abiding behavior. CJ-PMI should not be punished when their mental health symptoms impair functioning, rather punishments should be used only when criminalness is the root cause for one's behavior.

CJ-PMI must accept responsibility for their recovery. One way for CJ-PMI to accept responsibility is by asking for help when they are struggling with their recovery. Family members and significant others who are prosocial should be sought out and incorporated into relapse prevention plans. CJ-PMI are responsible for maintaining these external supports and should actively rely on these supports during periods of struggle. Finally, for recovery to occur CJ-PMI must be afforded recovery-oriented mental health and criminal justice services, the absence of which significantly reduces the individual's chance of full recovery and ultimately successful community reintegration.

Achieving recovery will ultimately result in CJ-PMI having increased good days, desistance from crime, reduced criminal and psychiatric recidivism, and increased prosocial behavior (e.g., independent living, work). Although recovery is the goal of this program, CJ-PMI will have their own personal goals and dreams (e.g., own one's own business, have a family, etc.), and these goals should be reinforced; however, it is the therapist's responsibility to relate these goals to the larger picture of recovery. CJ-PMI's personal goals and the overarching goal of recovery are essential for fostering each individual's commitment (responsibility) for change. Without this commitment to change, you, the therapist, will be impotent in spite of the best evidence-based practices for treating mental illness or criminalness.

How Do CJ-PMI Change?

Change begins with an effective relationship with service providers (including community providers following release from custody). However, it is the CJ-PMI's responsibility—and solely the CJ-PMI's responsibility—to change. Service providers, including probation/parole officers as well as mental health professionals, are available to assist CJ-PMI's efforts toward change (i.e., wellness, desistence from crime); however, the responsibility for remaining well resides with the CJ-PMI. To remain healthy and prosocial is critical to successful outcomes, and they are responsible for their well-being and achievement of life goals.

Mechanism and the Process of Change

Discussed in this section are content areas that have been previously shown to have some evidence in changing behavior. These do not operate in isolation, but together assist in changing behavior. As such, these are woven throughout the program, at times with a stronger emphasis on certain areas. With more evidence, certain areas may receive greater emphasis in its role as a mechanism of change. Thus, these principled content areas do not belong to this program, but to science.

New Attitudes and Cognitions

The relationship between how we think/process our thoughts and how we act is well-grounded. This is not a perfect relationship, but it is robust. The essence of the cognitive-behavioral approach is the identification of specific attitudes and cognitions associated with problematic emotions and non-productive behaviors. The goal, then, is to challenge the antisocial attitudes/cognitions and assist participants to alter them with more positive attitudes/cognitions or alter their behavior to be prosocial. This challenging of attitudes/cognitions works optimally in activities that extend into the client's real world. Clients need to over-learn information so that it becomes part of their natural behavior, and challenge criminal thinking as often and in as many different settings as possible.

New Skill Development

Developing new skills to change behavior works from the assumption that much change occurs through doing. The development of new skills is essential to a productive life. New prosocial skills are necessary to replace old maladaptive skills. Key skills involve assertion and communication skills. The development of new skills involves the ability to perceive and understand social cues and signals and then translate this into observable social action. More specifically, skill development involves avoidance procedures, effective and available reinforcers, and reinforcement contingencies. At one level, the goal is to develop social skills and coping strategies that are incongruent with crime.

New Responsibilities

Being responsible for one's productivity involves a process of self-reflection processes to assist one in identifying areas of need. These needs and deficits are identified through assessment and intervention activities (e.g., the use of the traffic light heuristic).

New Associations

Much behavior is guided by the people that are around us—those that we associate with. If those around us have a job, the likelihood that we will have a job is greatly increased. The development of new associates occurs through two venues. First is the attitudes/skills promoting the change of past criminal associates to prosocial associates. Second is the modeling that occurs with the program facilitator. This modeling of appropriate actions and a strengthening of relationships lays a foundation for long-term change.

Reduced Hedonistic Values

At the most basic level, clients need to consider the program's attempt to assist with change. Motivational interviewing strategies are used, but even with these, the participant needs to make a fundamental shift in their orientation of what should be considered for change. There is a strong use of cost–benefit ratios, and the listing of pros and cons for maintaining the unwanted thinking or pattern of behavior. A simple log of the hedonistic values will assist in change. Examining norms of the hedonistic values and how these relate to goal achievement works well. An aspect of this is the maintenance of therapeutic engagement.

5   Session Structure and Logistics

Modules contain an outline for each session within that module. For example, the second module, "Mental Illness and Criminalness Awareness," includes eight treatment sessions. This manual includes a treatment outline for each of these eight sessions. This outline was developed to guide you as you facilitate your CJ-PMI's learning, growth, and ultimate success in achieving their life goals. To assist you, each session follows a general format that is consistent throughout the manual.

First, treatment sessions will occur three times per week. This is our recommendation, but many agencies will find one or two sessions per week more feasible, whereas some facilities may be able to offer four or five sessions per week. Each session will last between 1 hr 30 min and 1 hr 50 min (the latter is the targeted session length, but some sessions will be shorter). Each session will be formatted in a manner to facilitate consistency so both you and the CJ-PMIs quickly learn what to expect in each session. Specifically, each session will be structured according to this schedule (time allotments are approximate and will differ according to session content and CJ-PMI needs):

Table 5.1 Suggested CLCO Session Schedule

Group Activity	Time Allotment (Approximate)
Interpersonal socializing and group warm-up, brief review of how group members are doing since the previous session	5–7 min
Review previous session content, address questions (questions related to previous content, homework, or program in general), and collect homework	10–15 min
Session content/work/group process	75–85 min
Assign homework	10–15 min

Group vs. Individual Therapy

Although *Changing Lives and Changing Outcomes* was designed for group work, this program can also be offered individually. Modifications will need to be made by the therapist as much of the therapeutic work, as designed, includes group work. The therapist will need to modify some handouts and worksheets for participants in one-to-one services.

Open vs. Closed Groups

There is evidence to support the benefits of open group therapy enrollment polices (see, e.g., Morgan & Flora, 2002); however, this program was developed to accommodate both open and closed enrollment policies. The program is developmental and sequential such that material heavily builds upon itself; however, closed enrollment is not fiscally or logistically feasible for all settings. Thus, we encourage open enrollment when necessary.

Open enrollment allows for more students to enter the program. All participants must complete Module I ("Preparing for Change") before entering an ongoing group. It is important that students who are entering an ongoing group (e.g., the middle of the program) *only* begin the program at the start of a module. That is, new participants should not join a group mid-module. This is so that there is less of a disruption for the other students in the class, and so that the new participants benefit from the developmental sequence of the module.

Group Size

It is recommended that groups be limited to 8–10 participants. As previously noted, this is a psychotherapy program and not a psychoeducational program; therefore we recommend group size be limited to that of a traditional psychotherapy group (i.e., 8–10 participants). Group size can certainly be increased or lowered to account for the experience and expertise of the therapist. For example, a therapist with years of correctional experience and years of experience providing psychotherapy groups may accommodate a group of 10–14 participants, whereas a therapist new to corrections or group therapy may lower admission to 6–8 participants.

6   Program Rules

Program rules are relevant if you are delivering *Changing Lives and Changing Outcomes* in a group format. It is imperative that CJ-PMI adhere to a set of basic guidelines and rules. It should be noted (stated explicitly for CJ-PMI) that a primary goal of this program is that CJ-PMI will accept responsibility for managing their illness and remaining crime-free, and each of these rules requires the responsible commitment of CJ-PMI. Violation of these rules continues a lifestyle of irresponsibleness and lack of commitment to recovery.

1. Confidentiality—You should define and explain confidentiality to the group. You should highlight for the participants the necessity of maintaining confidentiality for group members to talk and discuss issues openly. Trust is essential for group members to effectively help one another, and a lack of confidentiality destroys trust. Each participant will make a written and verbal commitment to the group that all discussions remain confidential.

2. Attendance—Participants are expected to attend all group activities. To successfully complete a module, a participant may miss no more than two sessions for modules of 10 sessions or more in length, or one session for modules of eight or fewer sessions. Under no circumstances will more than two absences be tolerated—more than two absences results in failure to complete the module.

3. Promptness—Participants are expected to be on time for each and every group session. Tardiness distracts the work of the group; thus, tardiness of greater than 10 minutes will be considered an absence, even if you attend the remainder of the group session (which is strongly encouraged—come if you are late even if you are counted absent). Note: the tardiness cutoff time should be developed with consideration of your setting. In some correctional settings, it is not atypical that participants will be 10 or more minutes late for an appointment (e.g., community corrections), but in other settings, 5 minutes might indicate significant and atypical tardiness (e.g., maximum security correctional facility).

4. Participation—Attendance is not sufficient. Remind participants they are expected to actively participate in group discussions. Each group session will begin with a brief question-and-answer period in which participants ask questions related to the session content, homework, and so forth.

5. Respect—Each group member is expected to treat one another with respect. Challenges of behaviors, beliefs, and opinions are necessary for change to occur; however, all interactions and communications, including challenges, will be communicated respectfully. Group members do not have to like one another or agree with one another, but they must interact in a respectful manner.

6. Homework—Remind participants that there are homework assignments for most sessions. They are responsible for completing *all* homework assignments.

7. Rules to be determined by participants—Group participants are afforded an opportunity to develop additional rules that they believe are important for their group. These additional rules are additive such that they are formally part of the group rules. They should be in writing and included in any discussion of group rules. Violation of these additional rules are dealt with in the same manner as other rule violations.

Note, we do not advocate for dismissing CJ-PMI from the program for rule violations with the exception of repeated breach of confidentiality. Rather, rule violations should be viewed as criminalness and dealt with therapeutically in the context of treatment sessions. Given findings that justice involved individuals benefit from being in treatment (i.e., dosage matters; Kroner & Takahashi, 2012), it would be detrimental and therapeutically counterproductive to dismiss participants for rule violations. CJ-PMI need to develop skills for following rule, so dismissing them without working on this aspect of their criminalness is contrary to the principles of *Changing Lives and Changing Outcomes.*

7 Certificates and Graduation Policies

Certificates of completion for each module and for the treatment program are included in Appendix A in the CJ-PMI Workbook. Certificates of completion will be distributed for each module successfully completed, and for the entire program, according to the following guidelines.

1. Module completion

    a. To successfully complete a module, a participant may miss no more than two sessions for modules of ten sessions or more in length, or one session for modules of eight or fewer sessions.

    - If a participant misses more than the allowed number of sessions per module, they may make up missed sessions by meeting individually with the therapist if the program is offered in a group format. If the program is offered individually, then the therapist may simply complete sessions in order such that no sessions are actually missed.

2. Program completion

    a. Participants successfully complete the program when they have successfully completed all modules.

Where the treatment program is offered in a group format, if a participant is unable to pass a module, they should continue to the next scheduled module with their fellow group members. They will need to repeat the failed module either with a subsequent group or individually with the treatment provider at the next available possible time in order to graduate from the entire program.

If the treatment program is being provided individually (i.e., one-to-one with a therapist), they should repeat the needed work in the module before proceeding to the next module.

Adjunctive Treatment Services

CJ-PMIs work and learn at varying rates. For example, a CJ-PMI with average intellectual functioning skills may learn and process information more quickly than a CJ-PMI with cognitive or reading deficits. Thus, individual counseling will be available on an as-needed basis to supplement group work, and an individual treatment plan should be developed for each participant. When individual counseling or tutoring is not sufficient for a participant to retain the essential components of each module, they should be encouraged to participate in the module a second time. In extreme cases, CJ-PMI may need two trials to complete the entire program.

8 Psychotherapy With CJ-PMI

Treatment with CJ involved individuals is difficult. They are often resistant to change, paranoid, and skeptical of the motives and intent of service providers, presenting with a myriad of complicated issues that are persistent (often lifelong) and not easily changed. Nevertheless, therapeutic programs and mental health services have proven effective for helping CJ involved individuals achieve more positive outcomes, including improved personal functioning and reduced recidivism. As such, we have preliminary data supportive of an evidence-based practice for working with CJ populations. Based on an aggregate of studies, we know that these evidence-based practices include targeting risk factors associated with criminal recidivism (i.e., the Central Eight risk factors; Andrews & Bonta, 2010) with intensive services that are cognitive-behavioral in orientation with structure integrated into the therapeutic environment, and with homework that is utilized to help CJ involved individuals apply new learning and skills in their real-world environment. It has also been recommended that treatments with those in the CJ system will be most effective when services are simplistic and utilize common, everyday learning heuristics, and when CJ involved individuals are required to overlearn treatment content so new behaviors become an ingrained part of their daily behavioral repertoire.

Changing Lives and Changing Outcomes utilizes each of these strategies to maximize treatment gains for CJ-PMI. Specifically, we structured this program to integrate cognitive-behavioral therapy, including structured learning activities, with an interpersonal process-oriented approach to group psychotherapy to maximize participant learning. We are consistent with best practices as the program is intensive (76 sessions for approximately 6 months of treatment if sessions are offered three times per week), and we include homework throughout the program (65 of the 76 sessions include out-of-session homework). Finally, we developed simple learning heuristics that are easily learned or already common to all participants (e.g., a stoplight to evaluate behaviors, associates) to simplify CJ-PMI's use of the skills and knowledge provided in this program.

9   Interpersonal Process-Oriented Group Psychotherapy

It should be noted that the interpersonal process-oriented approach described in this manual refers to the approach described by Dr. Irvin Yalom in his classic group psychotherapy text *Theory and Practice of Group Psychotherapy* (now in its 5th edition; see Yalom & Leszcz, 2005). We are not citing him for each statement or explanation, as that would detract from the readability; however, you should know that we are indebted to Dr. Yalom for his innovative group work, and the information described in chapters 9 and 10 is our summary of his intellectual work (unless otherwise cited).

For therapists that are not familiar with the interpersonal process approach to group psychotherapy, it is recommended that you read this chapter multiple times, as the more you practice and read the material here, the greater your skill development. Furthermore, given the complexity and quantity of educational information in this program, it may be easy to lose focus on the psychotherapeutic process and, in the words of doctoral student therapists, "you can get bogged down with the content and the focus can shift to solely didactic." Reading this chapter multiple times (including after you have initiated the treatment) will help you avoid this pitfall. Continuing education in interpersonal process-oriented group psychotherapy may also be beneficial.

The interpersonal process-oriented approach to group therapy as described here refers to an exploration of group members' interpersonal relationships with each other and their relationship to you (the facilitator). This exploration occurs within the group and remains the focus of the group; therefore the process of this approach is centered in the "here-and-now" (i.e., the present) and focuses on interpersonal relationships.

In describing this treatment approach, Yalom has indicated several key components which you must be aware of and attempt to implement to adequately facilitate this interpersonal process-oriented approach to group therapy. These components include (1) the 11 therapeutic factors of group work, (2) culture building and norm shaping, and (3) maintenance of a "here-and-now" focus. In addition, stages of group therapy and group dynamics will be discussed briefly.

Therapeutic Factors

Yalom has empirically identified eleven therapeutic factors based on the "intricate interplay of human experience" (p. 1) and that opens the pathway to therapeutic change. These eleven factors are: (1) instillation of hope, (2) universality, (3) imparting information, (4) altruism, (5) the corrective recapitulation of the primary family group, (6) development of socializing techniques, (7) imitative behavior, (8) interpersonal learning, (9) group cohesiveness, (10) catharsis, and (11) existential factors. The following is a description and therapeutic explanation of each of the 11 therapeutic factors.

Instillation of Hope

Hope is central to the therapy process. CJ-PMIs (and therapists) need to achieve and maintain hope that change is possible. Hope is necessary for therapeutic engagement, but also "faith in a treatment mode can in itself be therapeutically effective" (Yalom & Leszez, 2005, p. 4). As the group facilitator you must be able to communicate how this group approach will help CJ-PMIs. In addition, you should attempt to capitalize on CJ-PMI's hope in the efficacy of this treatment approach whenever possible (e.g., emphasize hope in early group sessions, reinforce positive expectations, educate when faced with negative preconceptions, and direct attention to improvements displayed during the course of the group).

Universality

CJ-PMI may enter therapy with the preconceived idea that they are alone with their problems and that others do not share similar difficulties. Although this is true to some extent, the disconfirmation of a participant's uniqueness may be a powerful sense of relief. That is, CJ-PMI learn that they are universally similar. It is assumed that as participants begin to share and learn of each other's similarities, they will become more trusting and open with one another. Your role is to aid in the development of group universality by pointing out group similarities. When CJ-PMI present with problems or goals that are similar, it is important that you indicate the universal nature of their issues. This may be most easily achieved during the first group session. As CJ-PMI begin to discuss their lives, you will help the group identify commonalties in their life histories, presenting problems, and treatment goals.

Imparting Information

This therapeutic factor includes both didactic instruction (e.g., psychoeducation) and direct advice (by the therapist as well as group members). In general, clients in interpersonal process-oriented groups do not highly value didactic instruction or advice giving, and Yalom discourages such practices;

however, you will be both implementing didactic instruction and providing direct advice to the participants (as this is a primary element of the cognitive-behavioral supplement to this treatment approach). Group members will also give advice to one another, especially in early stages of the group.

Although group members typically do not find the advice of other group members highly beneficial, advice giving serves a purpose. The process, rather than the content, is important as it implies and conveys mutual interest and caring. This is an important facet of group therapy, and CJ-PMI may benefit from acknowledging that they are interested in and care about one another.

Altruism

In group therapy, patients benefit from giving. CJ-PMI may particularly benefit from this factor as it may be one of the few times that he or she gives rather than takes. CJ-PMI may believe that they are a burden to others, and the experience that they can be helpful or of importance to others may be refreshing and may boost self-esteem. CJ-PMI in group therapy may be helpful to one another via providing support, reassurances, suggestions, insight, and sharing problems. Not infrequently, participants in group therapy will accept observations from other participants long before they accept your observations. You may be perceived as a cop or, at the least, a paid professional who is not from the real world, someone who cannot really understand them. Other CJ-PMI are real and understand their plight, and thus are more credible sources of information. Typically, CJ-PMI question the utility of group therapy asking questions such as "How can the blind lead the blind?" This resistance may be best explored through the therapeutic factor of altruism. A participant who says other participants are in the same position as him or herself and cannot possibly be of help to him/her is in effect saying "these participants are like me, and I have nothing of value to offer them." You can assist them in exploring their negative self-evaluation by helping them identify ways that they can be of assistance to the group. Others may vicariously benefit from this process exploration. In addition, it may prove beneficial to reflect the support you notice in group sessions.

It is important to note that therapists should take extra note of instances of altruism and actively identify such behaviors in the course of treatment, as many CJ-PMI harbor feelings of guilt and shame and often hold the belief that they are not needed or useful to others. Thus, actively identifying instances of altruistic behavior will be important for this population.

The Corrective Recapitulation of the Primary Family Group

Group therapy results in group dynamics that closely resemble familial dynamics. Many aspects of families are re-experienced in the therapy group: authority/parental figures, peer siblings, strong emotions, deep intimacy, and hostile and competitive feelings. Responses to other participants in the group will be similar to reactions to family members. Of therapeutic importance, however, is not that early family experiences or conflicts are merely relived; rather, that they are relived correctly. Your task is to find common ties between past and current feelings, thoughts, and behaviors, and to explore and challenge rigid interpersonal behaviors. You should assist CJ-PMI in identifying behaviors that are heavily influenced by early family experiences, and encourage them to experiment with new interpersonal behaviors in the group. The group should be a safe haven for them to try on new behaviors. Thus, when CJ-PMI can work out problems with you and the other members, they are actually working through unfinished business from previous relationships.

Development of Socializing Techniques

Group therapy provides an instant laboratory for the observation and development of social skills. The development of socializing skills in an interpersonal process-oriented group is a secondary gain as social skills training is not a focus of these groups; however, CJ-PMI may learn from feedback from others about their social behaviors. This may provide them with a unique and previously unexperienced opportunity of receiving direct feedback regarding interpersonal skills. In fact, members in one of the field testing groups specifically commented on the opportunity to provide and receive feedback from others in a safe environment of the treatment setting as being a new and innovative behavior and one they greatly appreciated.

It appears intuitively plausible that this feedback could only help CJ-PMI in their interpersonal relationships. Yalom (p. 17) emphasizes the potential benefits of this therapeutic factor when he states

> senior members . . . are attuned to process; they have learned how to be helpfully responsive to others; they have acquired methods of conflict resolution; they are less likely to be judgmental and more capable of experiencing and expressing accurate empathy.

Granted, a correctional population is not Yalom's typical clientele; however, it does not seem unreasonable to suggest that similar benefits may be encountered by CJ-PMI working in interpersonal process-oriented groups. Your task here is to aid participants in developing more functional social skills via modeling and/or feedback.

Imitative Behavior

We have all at one time or another imitated behaviors of others. Group therapy is no different, as participants will model their own behavior on the aspects of other group members or the facilitator. CJ-PMI in this group will likely "try on" bits and pieces of other people in group and then keep those behaviors that "fit" and discard qualities that are ill-fitting. Yalom articulates this point very succinctly when he writes about this process of trying on and discarding others' qualities or characteristics as beneficial, because finding out who we are not is important in finding out who we are.

Interpersonal Learning

Interpersonal learning is by far the most abstract and difficult to explain of all of Yalom's therapeutic factors. Interpersonal learning includes processes that are similar to individual therapy such as insight, working through transference, and the corrective emotional experience. To understand interpersonal learning as identified by Yalom, you must first be familiar with his view of the importance of interpersonal relationships, the corrective emotional experience, and the group as social microcosm.

Interpersonal relationships are important because we develop a sense of who we are based on the perceptions and reflections of others. The inmate code, for example, is a way of living life for some inmates that they can be proud of when facing their peers. They will develop a sense of self as an upstanding person based on the responses of others in the correctional population when adhering to the inmate code. With regard to interpersonal relationships, individuals have a tendency to distort perceptions of others (Yalom refers to these distorted perceptions as "parataxic distortions"). These distortions occur in response to facilitators as well as group members. For example, a chronically angry and resentful participant may perceive others as harsh and rejecting. If this projection can be identified and discussed in group, then he or she may be in a unique position to obtain consensual validation (i.e., obtain feedback from the group with regard to his or her self-evaluation).

It is assumed that the group will rekindle previous emotional experiences but that the participant will be allowed to experience a "corrective emotional experience." That is, participant growth may develop through self-disclosure of emotionally laden material and group feedback allows for reality testing. Five components appear of utmost importance with regard to the "corrective emotional experience": (1) CJ-PMI will take risks of expressing strong emotional reactions; (2) the group must support the participants' risk; (3) group process is examined; (4) inappropriate feelings and behaviors or avoided interpersonal behaviors are recognized; and (5) more honest and deeper interactions are facilitated. Again it should be noted that the emotional expression is not sufficient to promote change and that a cognitive component is essential for change to occur. You will need to assist the group by framing and/or making sense of the emotions exhibited in the group.

One of the primary benefits from interactive groups is that they facilitate a social microcosm of the group members. That is, with the passage of time, group members will display their pathologies. They will be themselves during group interactions. You do not need to ask about their pathologies, because they will display them for you and everyone else to see.

One of your most significant tasks will be to identify and subject to therapy those maladaptive interpersonal behaviors of group members and help them learn new ways of relating. Prior to turning the social microcosm to a therapeutic advantage, you must first identify group members' recurrent maladaptive patterns. Participants will elicit feelings from other group members, and you need to consider these feelings as data. If these are not the feelings that the participant desires to elicit, then a problem has been identified. Note that one response of another group member is insufficient data and you must seek confirmatory data. Consensual validation (feedback about one's self-evaluation) from the group must be obtained to truly aid in the identification of maladaptive interpersonal styles in each group member. With regard to group therapy in prisons, one complaint frequently voiced by participants in group psychotherapy is that the group and its interactions are not representative of the real world, that the group is artificial and contrived. It should be pointed out that while the group members meet only once a week, they are in a position to explore with great depth the life experiences and interpersonal functioning of one another. The kind of trust and honesty necessary to work together cannot possibly be considered artificial. There is nothing artificial about a CJ-PMI expressing anger with you or another participant.

Lastly, the therapeutic factor of interpersonal learning must include a discussion of insight. Insight is the discovery of something of importance about oneself, and may occur on at least four different levels:

1. CJ-PMI may develop an objective impression of their interpersonal style. They may learn how others view them.
2. CJ-PMI may develop an understanding of their interactional patterns.
3. CJ-PMI may develop an understanding of the motivations behind their interactional patterns. They may learn why they interact the way they do. For example, CJ-PMI may learn that they behave in certain ways to avoid perceived catastrophes (e.g., if I express my anger, I will end up in a fight; if I cry, I will be perceived by others as weak).
4. CJ-PMI may develop an understanding of how they became the way they are.

Group Cohesiveness

Group cohesiveness in its most basic form refers to the attractiveness of a group for its members. Defined more behaviorally, group cohesiveness refers to members' feelings of warmth and comfort in the group, feelings of belonging, valuing the group, and feelings of being valued, unconditionally accepted and supported by the other group members. Group cohesiveness appears to be a necessary component of group therapy, and a group of CJ-PMI, as well as any other group, should be able to develop this therapeutic factor. Group cohesiveness is not a stagnant process; rather, the cohesiveness of any group fluctuates with the circumstances of the group. However, some level of group cohesiveness must be maintained, or members are likely to leave the group.

CJ-PMI frequently come from impoverished backgrounds and unfortunately many experience few opportunities to join and function in a group. Although group cohesiveness may be slow to develop with this population, once CJ-PMI develop a sense of public esteem, increased self-esteem is sure to follow. Public esteem is critical to the efficacy of group therapy. The more significance a participant places on the group in his/her life, the more that participant will subscribe to the group norms and values, and the more inclined he or she will be to hear and accept group judgments.

Lastly, it is critical to the process of group therapy that you do not misinterpret group cohesiveness as comfort. Cohesive groups should be better able to develop and express anger and conflict. Hostility must be acknowledged and expressed to avoid covert hostility, which would significantly hinder the effectiveness of the group. Hostility in group therapy must be processed, and it is imperative that the conflicting group members establish a means of working together.

CJ-PMI may have a tendency to avoid open expression of anger and hostility; however, as the group facilitator you need to help the group identify and explore conflict via the open expression of anger. Be aware and prepare for the initial expression of anger to be directed at you. If the group members cannot trust you with their anger, how can they trust each other? This issue will be discussed in greater detail under the heading "stages of group therapy," but suffice to say for now that you should observe participant challenges or confrontations at some point in the early group development. You may be confronted about your lack of direction, your lack of care and concern, that you are only in the job for the money, that you are a cop, or that you are part of the system. If you do not deal with this open expression of anger (allow members to share their disappointment, anger, etc.) you will inadvertently establish a group norm discouraging the open expression of intense feelings.

Catharsis

Catharsis is the process of emotional experience and generally refers to expressing and discharging previously repressed emotions. It is generally accepted by most theorists and clinicians that catharsis is not sufficient to promote psychological change. As the facilitator, one of your tasks is to help the CJ-PMI get beyond the ventilation of feelings and attempt to add meaning or significance to the cathartic experience. You must facilitate the dual process of expressing feelings and then reflecting back on the process (this process is known as the self-reflective loop and is discussed in greater detail below). For example, you might ask a group member what it was like to share those feelings in the group just now. Catharsis is critical to group therapy: without it, the group would be a sterile intellectual discussion of ideas and thoughts, yet it is insufficient to promote change and must be supplemented by other therapeutic factors. In addition, this therapeutic factor allows CJ-PMI (possibly for the first time in their lives) to learn and be able to say what is bothering them. With regard to catharsis with CJ-PMI, please note that expression of affect is a relative experience. What one perceives as intense may not be the same as what others perceive as intense. Thus, if a relatively constricted participant expresses an affective response, consider the experience from that individual's experiential world.

Existential Factors

The existential factors refer to the search for purpose and meaning in life, and consist of five points:

1. "Recognizing that life is at times unfair and unjust";
2. "Recognizing that ultimately there is no escape from some of life's pain or from death";
3. "Recognizing that no matter how close I get to other people, I must still face life alone";
4. "Facing the basic issues of my life and death, and thus living my life more honestly and being less caught up in trivialities";
5. "Learning that I must take ultimate responsibility for the way I live my life no matter how much guidance and support I get from others" (p. 88).

In a general sense, these five existential factors emphasize awareness of death, freedom, isolation, the purpose of life, and the struggle with existence. This therapeutic factor is not grounded in techniques or strategies; instead it is an attitude or a way of viewing the world. Your task is to aid the participant in exploring his or her role in the world and his or her way of living life, rather his or her life is existing in prison or in the free world.

Integrating the Therapeutic Factors

As you read about the 11 therapeutic factors in this chapter, you probably developed a sense of those therapeutic factors that carry more weight with regard to the change process. Yalom would not disagree with you. For example, instillation of hope, in and of itself, does not facilitate change; however, it helps keep members in the group to allow other therapeutic factors to facilitate change. In addition, the therapeutic factors should not be considered individually, but collectively.

Each factor contributes and is critical to the process of change. If you think of the change process in a circular fashion, with change at the top and each factor leading in successively back to change, you can see that if any one factor is removed, the circle is broken. Thus, each factor is not necessarily a condition of change, rather a mechanism in the process of change. One of your goals for your group should be to facilitate the process of change by integrating the therapeutic factors as described earlier.

Culture Building and Norm Shaping

One of your tasks as the group facilitator is to develop a group that works as a "therapeutic social system" (Yalom & Leszcz, 2005, p. 109). That is, you are not the agent of change; the group is. It should be the group members who facilitate change for one another via the therapeutic factors, thus it is your task to establish a group culture that maximizes the effective therapeutic interactions. Granted, Yalom developed this theory for outpatient populations and not a correctional or forensic population; however, we submit that CJ-PMI can obtain some level of a therapeutic environment as described by Yalom. Your task is similar to the outpatient therapist's task, in that you must maximize the strengths of the group to facilitate an interactional group.

In building a therapeutic culture, group norms will evolve. Some of the norms of the group will be explicit (e.g., identified group rules as described below), while most will be implicit. You influence the type of norms that evolve. In fact, you cannot help but influence the development of group norms. You need to be conscious of your influence on group norms and attempt to establish norms that facilitate interactional group therapy. In developing group norms you will assume two basic roles: technical expert and model-setting participant.

As the technical expert, you do not need to rely on group exercises or gimmicks to develop therapeutic norms. Rather, you can rely on your knowledge and experience to actively facilitate the group norms.

You already possess the necessary techniques for the development of the desired norms. You simply need to be conscious of how you effect group norms and plan your strategy appropriately. Yalom gives the following examples which we believe adequately describe your task here:

> the leader must attempt to create an interactional network in which the members freely interact rather than directing all their comments to or through the therapist. To this end, therapists may implicitly instruct members in their pregroup interviews or in the first group sessions: they may, repeatedly during the meetings, ask for all members' reactions to another member or toward a group issue; they may wonder why conversation is invariably directed toward the therapist; they may refuse to answer questions or may even close their eyes when addressed; they may ask the group to engage in exercises that teach patients to interact—for example, asking each member of the group, in turn, to give his or her impressions of every other member; or therapists may, in a much less obtrusive manner, shape behavior by rewarding members who address one another—therapists may nod or smile at them, address them warmly, or shift their posture into a more receptive position.
>
> (2005, pp. 123–124)

As the model-setting participant, you shape group norms by example. You should attempt to model four basic functions: (1) honest and open communication, (2) appropriate restraint, (3) avoid overly self-disclosing too early in the group (i.e., avoid promiscuous self-disclosure), and (4) transparency (i.e., do not hide behind your role as group facilitator). To function as a model you must "join" the group. You will be expected to share with the group. You will not need to share identifying information (a process that can prove dangerous with this population); however, you should be willing to share your own interpersonal difficulties with the group. For example, if you find yourself in constant conflict with a particular participant, you can model trust and openness by exposing this conflict to the process of the group. You will model honest and open communication and transparency, but to do this you must be comfortable with yourself and allow yourself to come out from behind your role as facilitator. In effect, you become a group member who is subjected to interpersonal difficulties just like everyone else in the world. Finally, you should positively reinforce similar client behavior. Do not punish those who are less trusting and share only minimally. You should *reinforce* them for what they have shared, you can process their difficulty in opening up more to the group, you can engage in risk assessment of opening up, and you can encourage participants to share more, but do not act in a punitive manner to the amount or your perceived tardiness of their sharing. To do so will inadvertently reinforce negative feelings of sharing. The practice of reinforcing participants for what they have shared was reinforced by one of the field testing therapists, who noted "these individuals are so paranoid and distrusting . . . it takes up to 2–3 months before they finally get comfortable." So be proactive in your reinforcement of sharing and open dialogue. CJ-PMI will learn that sharing only leads to greater expectations of what one must share, and everyone will be afraid to be more open with the group.

Present-Centered Focus

As stated previously, present-centered refers to the focus on the interpersonal relationships within the group and occurs in the present. The focus on the here-and-now is of paramount importance in Yalom's theory and is a concept that you will need to be familiar and comfortable with to facilitate an interpersonal process-oriented group. For this reason, we contribute more detail to this concept than any other concepts in this theory. To implement a here-and-now focus, you need to know that this process occurs at two levels: the first is an experiential level, and the second is an "illumination of process" level.

At the experiential level, group members will experience feelings in the here-and-now. Some of these feelings will be strong and will be in reaction to other group members, the therapist, and the group at large. The focus of this portion of the group will be on these feelings. Identifying and sharing these feelings with the group will be one of your primary goals for each of the individual members. The events in meetings must take precedence over any other events (e.g., conflict with officers, problems with cellmates). That is not to say that other events in the individual's life are not to be discussed, however, the group focus must remain on intergroup behaviors. The here-and-now focus will remain incomplete without the second level, the illumination of process. That is, you must facilitate "process commentary" (i.e., explaining what you observed/heard happening in the group) on the events that occur in the here-and-now. Experiencing is insufficient to facilitate change; the experiencing must be accompanied by interpersonal learning which occurs through process commentary. Thus, you have two tasks: facilitate a here-and-now focus, and then lead the group in an exploration of the here-and-now behaviors. In effect, the group will perform a "self-reflective loop." The group will live in the here-and-now, and then reflect back on the behavior that occurred.

For purposes of this group, process will refer to the interpersonal relationships between group members. Process is not the same as content.

Content refers to the explicit meaning of statements, whereas process refers to underlying meanings.

To understand the process you need to consider the reason, *from an interpersonal perspective*, that group members make statements when they do, how they do, and to whom they do. In other words, why is a participant saying what s/he is saying, how s/he is saying it, and to whom s/he is saying it. This is the group process, and it is this process commentary that separates experiential group therapy from other social interactions.

Some techniques may aid you in activating a here-and-now focus; however, you are strongly encouraged not to rely on these techniques in a prescriptive format, rather to understand the purpose and intent behind the techniques. In so doing, you will then be in a position to initiate your own techniques that are consistent with your own individual style. First, it may help you to think in the here-and-now. Your focus should be on attempting to bring each group session, each event, into the here-and-now. Ask yourself questions such as how can I get this discussion into the here-and-now? This should be done as early as the first group session. For instance, after group introductions and initial discussion, you may interrupt the group with a process commentary. Yalom (2005, p. 157) provides the following narrated example:

> We've done a great deal here today so far. Each of you has shared . . . But I have a hunch that something else is going on, and that is that you're sizing one another up, each arriving at some impressions of the other, each wondering how you'll fit in with the others. I wonder now if we could spend some time discussing what each of us has come up with thus far.

As you can see from this example, you can directly influence a here-and-now focus. You will attempt to adjust the focus from the external, abstract, and impersonal to the internal, specific, and personal. Encourage the use of the first person rather than the third person. Identify when group members are talking to you and encourage group communication. Other examples of moving the focus to a here-and-now focus will be presented in the training sessions.

Another strategy is to provide feedback on how to ask and give feedback to and from other group members. It may be necessary for participants to occasionally check out their beliefs with the group. Help them avoid group questions such as "Do you like me?" in favor of more effective questions such as "What is it about me that you like most and least?" This type of activity promotes process commentary and includes the following sequence:

1. A description of behavior. CJ-PMI learn to see themselves as others see them.
2. Here is the impact of your behavior on others. CJ-PMI learn how their behavior makes others feel.
3. Here is the impact of your behavior on others attitudes toward you. CJ-PMI learn how others feel about them as a result of their behavior.
4. Here is the impact of your behavior on your attitude toward yourself. CJ-PMI learn how their behavior influences their own attitude about themselves.

When initially inquiring about intergroup relations, you will receive resistance from the group. They will say something to the effect that they like all of the group members the same. It may be important for you to accept these defenses initially, but stay with the task, continue to probe and explore, and do not hesitate to model interpersonal communications. For example, after a long silence you may initiate process commentary by asking for the thoughts of the group members that were "unsaid." You can then model this behavior by sharing your own thoughts that occurred during the silence.

At times it may occur to you that things are going unsaid as the group is nearing the end. You may have the members imagine that the group has just ended and they are walking back to their cells. Ask them what disappointments they would have about that session.

Also, do not hesitate to wonder about how group discussions relate to the group session (e.g., if they are discussing the frustration of inmates or patients in the facility, wonder aloud if that is how they are feeling in the group). Your wondering may or may not be accurate, but either way, you facilitate a here-and-now focus.

Once you have established a here-and-now focus, you must then use this process therapeutically (i.e., process illumination). The illumination of process consists of four stages: (1) participant recognition of their behavior, (2) participant understanding of the effects of this behavior, (3) determination of participants' satisfaction with their behavior, and (4) change in behavior. To facilitate these stages you must first be able to recognize process. This is a skill that generally occurs with experience, and you may or may not have had opportunities to develop this skill. Some specific examples will be provided to aid you, as needed, in the recognition of process.

Establishing a process orientation within the group is as difficult and maybe more so than establishing a here-and-now focus; however, another one of your tasks will be to facilitate an environment that accepts a process orientation. In doing so, you are encouraged to attempt to facilitate participant learning via their own route. That is, you may have to hold on to some process commentary until you are able to find a method that allows the participant to obtain their own insight. This will carry much more weight than any brilliant interpretation that you as a facilitator can offer. This is not an easy task, and as the time frame for this group is relatively short (especially by Yalom's standards), you are encouraged to weigh the time limits against the clinical utility of making an interpretation.

When you choose to illuminate the group process, you are advised to consider how you can aid the participant in hearing your process commentary. Some basic concepts are suggested here. First and most obvious, CJ-PMI may hear your interpretations more clearly if they are framed in a supportive manner. Second, avoid the temptation to label or classify (e.g., antisocial, narcissistic, uncaring). A statement first describing some positive aspect of their group behavior followed by an observation and interpretation of the ineffective or aversive group behavior may be more easily heard by the participant. Third, be observant of "moments of truth." That is, there are times when in an instant of openness a participant discloses some truth that will provide you with therapeutic leverage at a later point in the group. For example, a participant may state that they would like to develop more intimate relationships with others. By remembering this statement you may be in a position to use his stated desire in making a process commentary to how his intergroup behavior effects his relationships with others in the group.

Stages of Group Psychotherapy

Yalom identifies three stages of group therapy that all groups must obtain in order to become a functional therapeutic group. These stages include the initial stage; the conflict, dominance and rebellion stage; and the development of group cohesiveness stage. These stages are not clearly defined as to when or how a particular group will progress through each stage, but as the facilitator you should be able to recognize and process with the group the stages as they occur.

The initial stage (also referred to by Yalom as the "in or out" stage) is characterized by four phases. First, there must be an orientation to the group. You can facilitate this phase by discussing the purpose of the group, expectations of group members, and structure of the group. Second, it is normal for group members to be hesitant about group participation and self-disclosure. Trust has not yet formed, and the participants will continue to seek approval from the group rather than openly discuss their life struggles. Third, the group will experience a "search for meaning" phase. They will attempt to make sense of the group, ask and explore how the group will help them, question how much they really want to share, and attempt to find a role within the group. Finally, there will be a dependency phase. Here the participants will look for structure, typically from you. They will seek you out for direction, approval, and acceptance, and you will see many of the group statements directed to you. You can exert great influence at this point and must remember that you are attempting to establish therapeutic norms as described previously.

The second stage of group therapy is the conflict, dominance, and rebellion stage (which Yalom also refers to as the "top-bottom" stage). Here the group shifts focus from approval and acceptance to conflict, dominance, and power. A group hierarchy will likely emerge as CJ-PMI jostle for position within the group. In this stage, they are becoming more real, and you will begin to see who the group members really are. Controlling and dominant participants will attempt to assume control in the group, while more passive individuals will allow the group to be directed by others. The CJ-PMI are allowed to be a little more real because in this stage they are becoming more comfortable with one another. The first sign that the second stage is occurring is the emergence of conflict. This conflict will typically not present itself in a hostile or aggressive fashion. Rather, subtle disagreements will become evident. This is the group's method of "testing the waters" for the acceptance of conflict. As stated previously, group conflict will invariably be directed to you first. If they can not express conflict with you, the facilitator, how can they trust to express conflict with one another? A group without conflict will be like a marriage without conflict—boring, distant, detached, and unreal. You must be prepared to accept conflict, no matter how great or small the challenge, because the group's challenge of you is essential to the life of the group. As such, you must not only permit but encourage confrontation (e.g., reinforce challenges) directed at you. Rest assured, the group will save you and eventually switch the focus of the challenges from you to one another.

The development of group cohesiveness is the third and final stage of group therapy identified by Yalom. He has also referred to this stage as a "close-far" stage. This stage is characterized by an increase in trust, self-disclosure, and group cohesion. The focus typically shifts from a conflictual process to one of intimacy. This stage permits the emergence of the real person and secrets are commonly shared. The group develops the cohesion necessary for intimate work to occur. Group cohesion is a relative term. CJ-PMI may develop a strong sense of cohesion that is not easily recognized by facilitators experienced with groups that have achieved more intimate levels. You should caution against harboring high expectations, yet allow yourself to develop a sense for and some expectations for intimacy to occur within the group. You should acknowledge with the group their movement toward intimacy and closeness and reinforce behaviors that initiate this process.

Some Notes About Group Dynamics

You already have a good sense about group dynamics, both from experience and from reading the previous sections of this manual. In this section, we want to clarify or describe some of the important group dynamics identified by Yalom that you should be aware of but that were not identified earlier. These dynamics include group maintenance, group resistance, and problem patients.

Group maintenance will be one of your primary tasks once the group has begun. You must identify and deter any threats to group cohesiveness. Frequent tardiness, subgrouping, and scapegoating are examples of processes that can negatively impact group cohesiveness. You need to monitor the cohesiveness of the group, and it may be necessary at times to delay work on an individual's problems for the betterment of the group. For example, if a new participant enters the group and is unacknowledged while another group member immediately engages in a dialogue of his or her problems, you should consider stopping this member and processing with the group the new member's presence and the group's lack of acknowledgment to him or her. Again, you should attempt to confront this behavior in a non-punitive manner. For example, you may ask the speaking participant how he or she thinks the new participant is feeling in the group at that point.

Group resistance is common in any group therapy, but this issue is even more salient when working with a CJ population. You may frequently observe group members becoming resistant (generally defined as pain avoidance) to you, to other group members, or to the group at large. When this occurs, your task is to help the participant see through their resistance to be able to hear the message they are receiving. It is only then that they can accurately confirm or disconfirm a message. For example, it is likely at some point in your group that a group member will make an observation or interpretation to another group member who in turn becomes defensive and resistant to this message. You may encourage the participant to listen to the message by acknowledging their ability to defend against or counter the message, but point out that in doing so, he or she is unable to accurately hear the message and is unable to discern which parts of the message are actually true for him or her.

Problem patients exist in all groups, and your CJ group will be no different. Common problem patient presentations include the monopolist (talks a great deal in group), the silent patient (talks rarely), the boring patient (offers detailed stories that stay at a surface level), and most common for your group, the characterological difficult client (personality problems/disorders). These group members will test your patience as well as your ability to facilitate a therapeutic group; however, you may be helped by understanding that these are interpersonal problems. You will be unsuccessful in your attempts to confront or challenge this behavior, but you may find success in interpretations of how the behavior affects their interpersonal relationships. Furthermore, you will be especially effective if you can aid the participant in identifying how the effects of his or her behavior actually contradict what s/he desires in interpersonal relationships.

Summary of an Interpersonal Process-Oriented Approach to Group Therapy

This approach to group psychotherapy with CJ-PMI will incorporate Yalom's (2005) interpersonal process-oriented theory. The foundation of this treatment will consist of 11 therapeutic factors: instillation of hope, universality, imparting information, altruism, the corrective recapitulation of the primary family group, development of socializing techniques, imitative behavior, interpersonal learning, group cohesiveness, catharsis, and existential factors. These factors do not facilitate change independently; rather, they should be implemented collectively into the treatment process. One of your tasks is to facilitate a culture and develop norms that are conducive to interpersonal exploration. This interpersonal exploration should occur in the here-and-now, as group members will react with emotion to the group members, the therapist, and the group as a whole; however, this is not sufficient for change. You must facilitate a self-reflective loop where group members share their feelings and then reflect back on this experience with the group. Lastly, you should be aware of the group stages your group members may progress through, including the initial stage (characterized by group orientation, hesitant participation, a "search for meaning," and dependency); the conflict, dominance and rebellion stage (characterized by a focus shift to issues of conflict, dominance, and power); and the development of group cohesiveness stage (characterized by increased trust, self-disclosure, and group cohesion).

By now you should have a sense of your task when facilitating an interpersonal process-oriented approach to group psychotherapy with CJ-PMI. It is hoped that the modules and session outlines prepare you with the knowledge and content for facilitating a therapeutic environment that is rich in opportunity for CJ-PMI to develop greater understanding of their mental illness and criminalness, as well as develop the skills and knowledge to live more productive lives. The avenue to this change lies in the psychotherapeutic process as described earlier (e.g., therapeutic factors, here-and-now process, challenging of non-productive beliefs and attitudes). As you begin to facilitate *Changing Lives and Changing Outcomes*, you are advised to maintain your present-centered awareness with focus on how CJ-PMI's behaviors do and do not lead to responsible and prosocial choices and behaviors. The modules and therapeutic strategies of *Changing Lives and Changing Outcomes* will be much less potent if you are unable to bring the modules and learning back to the issue of the CJ-PMI accepting responsibility for their choices, their behaviors, and their outcomes—in other words, they are solely responsible for their recovery.

10 Bi-adaptive Model of Intervention

Bi-adaptive Model of Change

The Bi-adaptive model posits an overlap between mental illness and criminalness within a person. This is supported by shared problems between criminalness and mental illness. The three areas of emotional dysregulation, impaired social functioning, and skill deficits are shared with criminalness and mental illness. Even with these shared problem areas, the main features of criminalness are what contributes to antisocial negative outcomes. The major role of mental illness is to confound the clinical picture. Pathological expressions will mask the mechanisms of acting out behaviors. Addressing and treating mental illness may have little impact on antisocial negative behaviors. As an example, with some samples depression will have an inverse relationship with acting out behaviors, and with others there will be a positive relationship. Thus, in relation to criminalness, mental illness will not be clearly related to antisocial negative outcomes.

Treatment Context

Changing Lives and Changing Outcomes includes a comprehensive and structured treatment manual that provides clinicians a guide for treating CJ-PMI. We emphasize *guide* because we submit that clinicians are ultimately responsible for the care their patients receive, and therapists must have flexibility with regard to the treatments they provide.

Nevertheless, *Changing Lives and Changing Outcomes* offers a treatment plan for each session with specific structured exercises for both in-group and out-of-group work (homework) designed to teach objectives each session. The program incorporates psychosocial rehabilitation and Risk-Need-Responsivity models, cognitive-behavioral theory, and a social learning paradigm to facilitate change. An important component of this intervention is that the manual was designed to be cumulative in nature, to facilitate continuity of modular intervention, such that knowledge accumulation and skill development builds on previous modules;

however, one strength of this intervention is administrative flexibility. That is, the entire intervention (i.e., nine modules) can be delivered or, given time constraints, service providers may select modules they deem most appropriate. The manual was designed for flexibility to allow service providers the option to implement the program with individual clients or in a group setting.

It is recommended that CJ-PMI attend three treatment sessions per week. Therapeutic services for individuals convicted of crimes are most successful when the services are intensive (Gendreau, 1996), and three sessions per week maximizes the learning opportunities and facilitates commitment to mastering module content. Each session is designed to last between 1 hr 30 min and 2 hrs, with the target session length of 1 hr 50 min.

As noted earlier, *Changing Lives and Changing Outcomes* includes nine therapeutic modules delivered in 76 sessions. Each module targets a specific problem or concern for CJ-PMI, includes pre-post testing sessions for the administration of outcome data, and a content examination. The treatment modules and primary therapy components are summarized below and presented in the order to be facilitated:

1. *"Preparing for Change" module* (three sessions). *CLCO* begins with a modified motivation to change treatment component. The "Preparing for Change" module is designed to motivate participants to assume responsibility for change and attainment of goals. Motivational interviewing strategies have shown to be effective for clients ambivalent about change (Miller & Rollnick, 1999). Furthermore, a positive commitment to change is associated with positive treatment results (Miller & Tonigan, 1996; Prochaska, DiClemente, & Norcross, 1992). Thus, prior to participating in the treatment modules, participants will complete three sessions specifically assessing readiness to change and enhancing CJ-PMI's commitment to change. In these three sessions the client's life goals are articulated and quantified, benefits of the *Changing Lives and Changing Outcomes* intervention are outlined, benefits of improved mental health and desistence from crime emphasized, and the five stages of change are outlined. Logistically, the motivation to change treatment component will include three group sessions over the course of one week. It is worth highlighting that, consistent with best correctional practices (Howells & Day, 2007; McGuire, 2003), strategies of motivational interviewing are interwoven throughout each module to emphasize and facilitate CJ-PMI commitment to positive change.

2. *"Mental Illness and Criminalness Awareness" module* (eight sessions). This module is designed to facilitate CJ-PMI's understanding and recognition of their psychiatric symptomatology and criminal propensity, particularly with regard to their mental health and

prosocial functioning. The principles guiding this module are consistent with principles of IMR and, consistent with the theoretical orientation of the bi-adaptive intervention, incorporating a social-cognitive learning model to facilitate CJ-PMI awareness. By developing awareness of psychiatric symptomatology and their specific mental illness, as well as their criminal propensities, CJ-PMI will be better equipped to utilize subsequent modules aimed at behavioral change to facilitate improved outcomes, including reduced psychiatric states and criminal recidivism (e.g., improved psychiatric functioning, more good days, fewer disciplinary infractions).

3. *"Thoughts and Attitudes" module* (13 sessions). This module is designed to facilitate a process of learning to identify, evaluate, and modify thinking and cognitive attitudes that contribute to criminalness and perpetuate impaired mental health functioning. CJ-PMI think differently than non-CJ-PMI (Walters, 1990; Yochelson & Samenow, 1976; Yochelson & Samenow, 1977), and the premise for this module is that "how people think has a controlling effect on how they act" (Bush & Bilodeau, 1993, p. 1). In other words, it is the way a person construes (thinks about) a situation that influences their feelings and behaviors (Beck, 1964; Beck, 1970). Thus, the foundation for this treatment component is a cognitive model (Beck, 1995) that applies to CJ-PMI as thinking styles and attitudes are common to criminal behavior, as well as impaired mental health functioning. Specifically, cognitive restructuring (cognitive-behavioral techniques for altering one's thoughts) will be used to facilitate changes in thoughts and beliefs that increase risk for criminal behavior, as well as thoughts and beliefs that contribute to negative feelings and dysfunctional behavior.

4. *"Medication Adherence" module* (five sessions). This module is designed to educate CJ-PMI about the necessity of maintaining a regular psychopharmacological treatment regimen. The focus of this module is on educating group participants on the biological mechanisms of schizophrenia, bipolar disorder, and major depressive disorder; the necessity of treating these disorders pharmacologically; and the benefits and side effects of various types of medications. Participants will also be educated about how to communicate with their physicians regarding their medications, specifically side effects they encounter, as well as coping strategies for undesirable side effects. This module relies primarily on a psychoeducational approach with the inclusion of homework assignments designed to integrate module content into the individual's everyday world.

5. *"Coping With Mental Illness and Criminalness" module* (eight sessions). This module is designed to educate CJ-PMI about managing their problems, including problems related to mental health functioning and criminalness. The focus of this module is on identifying

early warning signs of relapse (mental health and criminal), developing a relapse prevention plan for mental illness and criminalness, identifying the need for early interventions, coping with persistent symptoms of mental illness (e.g., cognitive process, mood disturbance) and criminalness (e.g., proneness to boredom, antisocial attitudes), and developing healthy and prosocial habits. This module relies primarily on a psychoeducational approach with the inclusion of homework assignments designed to integrate module content into the individual's everyday world.

6. *"Emotions Management" module* (10 sessions). This module covers the emotions of anxiety, depression, and anger. The content of the module deals with these content areas as both antecedents of criminal behavior and as a disorder in which the status can be improved. Areas of depression and anxiety have shown an association with violence among patients, but anger made an independent contribution to the prediction of future violence (Skeem et al., 2006). Although anger is not a formal diagnosis, this area has repeatedly been associated with violence and negative outcomes (Novaco, 1994; McNiel, Eisner, & Binder, 2003; Monahan & Steadman, 2001). Reducing the impact of each of anxiety, depression, and anger can be accomplished through the use of the thoughts/feelings, habits, and environment model. A strong emphasis is placed on the skills in each of these three areas that will assist in the reductions of the targeted behavior.

7. *"Associates" module* (10 sessions). This module employs social-cognitive learning theory as the theoretical underpinning to explain and change antisocial behavior. Consistent with social-cognitive learning theory, our thoughts and feelings, our habits (past behavioral repertoire), and our environment interact to contribute to our behavior. Our associates provide the social support (reinforcement) for the expression of our behavior and attitudes. The group process therefore seeks to identify and change the social reinforcement that results in offending behavior, including behaviors counterproductive to positive mental health. Thus, we use these four influences (thoughts/feelings, habits, environment, and associates) to demonstrate for the CJ-PMI how these four influences contributed to their current involvement in the criminal justice system and deteriorated mental health functioning over a lifetime; and, more importantly, how they can be used to improve the CJ-PMI situation to achieve positive outcomes.

8. *"Community Skills Development" module* (nine sessions). This module is designed to facilitate participants' development of problem-solving skills, social and recreational skills, and vocational/housing skills. The problem-solving skills curriculum teaches a five-stage problem-solving strategy developed by D'zurilla and Goldfried (1971). The five stages are (1) general orientation, (2) problem definition and formulation,

(3) generation of alternatives, (4) decision making, and (5) verification. Group and homework exercises are incorporated to facilitate participants' use of the strategy. The social and recreational skills section of this module educates CJ-PMI about expected forms of behavior (prosocial behavior), basic communication skills (including verbal and non-verbal communications), and prosocial recreational activities. The curriculum will include role-playing for the development of effective skills. The vocational/housing skills section of this module educates participants about basic job/house finding skills (including where to obtain information about available jobs/housing, applying for employment/housing, etc.), and utilizes role-playing and homework exercises to help participants develop discussed skills (e.g., development of a resume, mock interviews).

9. *"Substance Abuse" module* (10 sessions). This module aims to assess the level of substance use, examine antecedents to use, and reduce substance use. As noted by Drake, Wallach, and McGovern (2005), the development of a sense of meaning is important to changing substance use patterns among clients with severe mental illness. The module begins by examining the client's life goals and how reduced substance use can assist the client in attaining his/her goals. Based on the effectiveness of using readiness to change with substance use patients (Connors, Walitzer, & Dermen, 2002; Williams et al., 2006), two sessions are used to facilitate readiness for change. The contributors to substance use are examined through the thoughts/feelings, habits, and environment heuristic. The last five sessions develop skills for changing substance use patterns. Refusal skills are covered, along with skills in changing thoughts/feelings, habits, and environments as they relate to substance use. The importance of environmental issues, such as housing, has been highlighted by Drake et al., (2005). Finally, the client's antecedents and skills are summarized in a written self-management plan.

Although the proposed intervention is cumulative, such that it was designed for CJ-PMI to complete the intervention in the order described, it is flexible to allow for open enrollment. Thus, treatment dropouts or non-completers can be replaced by enrolling new participants at the beginning of the next scheduled module. For example, if a client terminates participation, is relocated to another facility, or completes their sanctioned sentence in the middle of a treatment module, a new participant will be enrolled at the beginning of the next module.

11 Assessment

Assessment is integral to the therapeutic process. It is essential to identify CJ-PMI risk for relapse (including both psychiatric and criminal relapses) as well as to guide treatment planning. Furthermore, in *Changing Lives and Changing Outcomes*, assessment is critical to visually show CJ-PMI their problem areas (e.g., criminal thinking). Thus, assessments will be administered throughout the program.

We have elected to use a pre-post assessment process. That is, we will assess participants before (pre) they start the treatment program, as well as after (post) they complete the program. In addition, we utilize a pre-post modular quiz to assess content mastery from each module. Thus, we recommend you administer a battery of assessment measures pre-post for the entire treatment program, as well as pre-post quizzes for eight of the treatment modules (we do not have a modular quiz for the "Preparing for Change" module). Chapter 12 includes a list of the assessment measures and administration schedule for both the pre-post program assessment, as well as the pre-post module assessment.

> **NOTE** If you do not elect to administer a battery of measures to assess treatment change, you will need to administer two tests for use during the treatment program. Specifically, you will need to administer the Psychological Inventory of Criminal Thinking Styles–Short Form (PICTS-SF) and the Measure of Criminal Attitudes and Associates (MCAA) for the "Thoughts and Attitudes" module. These measures are included in Appendix B in the CJ-PMI Workbook. The remainder of the measures we recommended are available as outlined in the description of each measure to follow.

Modular Quizzes

Modular quizzes will be used to assess for client content acquisition, that is, are clients learning the content presented in the modules? To assess knowledge acquisition, we have pre-post quizzes for each module except Module I, "Preparing for Change." Each quiz will be given during the first and last session of each module as specified in the treatment plan for each module throughout this manual. Quizzes and scoring keys are provided in Appendix C in the CJ-PMI Workbook.

12 Recommended Measures

We recommend the following measures because this battery of assessments provides a broad assessment of psychiatric, CJ-PMI, and general mental health functioning and outcomes. Also, it is important to note that these measures are all in the public domain (i.e., at no cost to you). Although we are using these measures in our assessment package, we encourage you to consider your assessment needs (client, agency, and fiscal) in selecting an assessment package that best suits your assessment interests and needs. On average, these measures take CJ-PMI individuals approximately 90 min to complete.

- The DSM-5 Self-Rated Level 1 Cross-Cutting Symptom Measure (DSM-5 Symptom Measure; American Psychiatric Association, 2013) is a 23-item self-report brief screening tool that assesses symptom presentation in relation to potential DSM-5 diagnoses. You can access this measure at https://www.psychiatry.org/File%20Library/Psychiatrists/Practice/DSM/APA_DSM5_Level-1-Measure-Adult.pdf.
- The Recovery Assessment Scale (RAS, Giffort, Schmook, Woody, Vollendorf, & Gervain, 1995) is a 41-item self-report measure that assesses the individual's sense of recovery through domains such as goal orientation, self-confidence, hope, reliance on others, and life-view. You can access this measure online via the Australian Mental Health Outcomes and Classification Network.
- The Psychological Inventory of Criminal Thinking Styles–Short Form (PICTS-SF; Walters, 2006) is a 35-item self-report measure that assesses thought patterns associated with criminal behavior. See participant workbook for a copy of this measure.
- The Measure of Criminal Attitudes and Associates (MCAA; Mills Kroner, & Forth, 2002) is a two-part self-report measure that evaluates criminal associates and antisocial attitudes. See participant workbook for a copy of this measure.

- The Medication Adherence Rating Scale (MARS; Thompson, Kulkarni, & Sergejew, 2000) is a 10-item self-report measure that assesses attitudes about medications and medication-taking behavior. You can access this measure at http://www.easacommunity. org/files/Medication%20Adherence%20Scale.pdf.
- The Positive and Negative Affect Schedule (PANAS; Watson, Clark, & Tellegen, 1988) is a 20-item self-report measure of positive and negative affect. You can access this measure at https://booksite.elsevier.com/9780123745170/Chapter%203/ Chapter_3_Worksheet_3.1.pdf.
- The Brief Situational Confidence Questionnaire (BSCQ; Breslin, Sobell, Sobell, & Agrawal, 1999) is an 8-item self-report measure that assesses self-confidence to resist either heavy alcohol or heavy drug use. You can access this measure at http://www.nova.edu/gsc/ forms/appendix_d_brief_situational_confidence_questionnaire.pdf.

It is also recommended that the assessment battery include a measure of client satisfaction in order to better understand the program, its utility, and the providers. There are several client satisfaction measures available for purchase, or items can be created by the provider to meet this need (e.g., How satisfied are you with the program? How satisfied are you with the services you received?).

Table 13.1 Schedule for Measure Administration

	Pre-treatment	*Module Completion*	*3-Month Mid-treatment*	*Treatment Completion*	*3 or 6 Months Post-treatment*
DSM-5 Symptom Measure	*		*	*	*
RAS	*		*	*	*
PICTS-SF	*		*	*	*
MCAA	*		*	*	*
MARS	*		*	*	*
PANAS	*		*	*	*
BSCQ	*		*	*	*
Module Quizzes	*	*			
Behavioral Data	TBD		TBD	TBD	TBD

Definitions

DSM-5 Symptom Measure = DSM-5 Self-Rated Level 1 Cross-Cutting Symptom Measure

RAS = Recovery Assessment Scale

PICTS-SF = Psychological Inventory of Criminal Thinking Style–Short Form

MCAA = Measure of Criminal Attitudes and Associates

MARS = Medication Adherence Rating Scale

PANAS = Positive and Negative Affect Schedule

BSCQ = Brief Situational Confidence Questionnaire (Substance Abuse)

Module Quizzes = Module quizzes can be administered all at once (all eight quizzes at one time) prior to the initiation of treatment or at the beginning of each module as is specified throughout the treatment manual.

Behavioral Data = Session attendance and participation, homework completion, quality of homework completion, time spent in segregation, disciplinary infractions, other institutional markers (note, a Microsoft Excel Spreadsheet for tracking session data (attendance, participation, homework data) is available on the CLCO Participant Workbook website (www.routledge.com/cw/Morgan).

Pre-treatment = Administered prior to the initiation of treatment services.

3-Month Mid-treatment = Administered 3 months after initiated treatment.

Treatment Completion = Administered prior to the participant discontinuing treatment.

3 or 6 Months Post-treatment = Administered 3 or 6 months after participant discontinues treatment.

13 Module I
Preparing for Change

The aim of this module is to engage the CJ-PMI, facilitating the positive benefits of participating in the treatment program. Building the motivation to change is found by exploring the participants' life goals. We offer this program to CJ-PMI as one way of successfully attaining life goals. Life goals is your *hook* from which you will engage your participants in the change process outlined throughout this program.

Among their life goals is their desire to get out of and stay out of a correctional environment, along with job or family aspirations. Most individuals in the criminal justice system identify the goal of remaining crime-free as their first priority. In addition to increasing the initial motivation for change, the "Preparing for Change" module can assist CJ-PMI stuck at a stage of change to move on or to go back to a previous stage of change. Engaging CJ-PMI, via motivational interviewing techniques, will impact the participant's evaluation of crime as worthwhile, perceptions of current life problems, anticipation of re-offending, and general attitudes to offending. The incorporation of motivational interviewing techniques into preparing the CJ-PMI for change will encourage those who are resistant or ambivalent about change to actively participate in change.

Content

The Motivational Interviewing Component includes three sessions to engage participants to develop person goals related to a crime-free lifestyle.

Session 1 explores the participant's difficulties and introduces the participant to the need to define their own life goals.

Session 2 assists the participant to define their own life goals and introduce the idea that the program will show them how to get from their current place to their life goals.

Session 3 assists the participant to develop personal goals. It will assist in identifying steps to achieving goals, by identifying steps, resources, and sources of help.

Treatment Process

Although the theoretical orientation of the *Changing Lives and Changing Outcomes* program integrates cognitive-behavioral and social-learning paradigms, the focus in this module is insight gained through education. To accomplish this goal, participants will attend three psychoeducational sessions. As the process for this module is psychoeducational in nature, each session is delivered with a cycle of content, in-class work, information handouts, and homework. The goal of the Motivational Interviewing module is to use both directive and non-directive questions, reflective listening, affirmation, and summaries to assist the participant in preparing for change.

Treatment Goals

The overarching treatment goal of the Motivational Interviewing Component is to place a CJ-PMI in a stronger position to have positive attitudes toward changing through the subsequent modules. These goals will help you, the therapist, to engage participants in the change process. In this module, participants should develop goals that will be used throughout the program to keep them on task (these goals are reviewed at the beginning of each module).

Session 1: Assessment of Client Difficulties and Developing Goals

Objective

This session will:

1. Build rapport with the participant
2. Assess the difficulties the participant had or is currently experiencing
3. Gain permission to change some things that contribute to his/her difficulties

The primary objective of the session is to explore the participant's difficulties and to introduce to the participant the need to define their own life goals.

Materials

1. Blackboard or whiteboard (with chalk or markers) or flip chart (with markers)
2. HANDOUT 1: Rules of the Pool
3. WORKSHEET 1: Personal Problems
4. HOMEWORK 1: Benefits of Change
5. Treatment Readiness Questionnaire

Session Content

1. **Welcome participants and group member introductions (summarize commonalities—Universality)**

   a. Basic demographics (where from, relationship status, children, occupational status, etc.)

   b. Criminal history (years incarcerated, index offense, length of prison/probation/parole sentence, etc.)

   c. Mental health history (current diagnosis, medications, previous hospitalizations, psychotherapy experience).

2. **Discuss program summary**

   a. Eight modules with one treatment component

   - Preparing for Change module
   - Mental Illness and Criminalness Awareness module
   - Thoughts and Attitudes module
   - Medication Adherence module
   - Coping With Mental Illness and Criminalness module
   - Emotions Management module
   - Associates module
   - Community Skills Development module
   - Substance Abuse module.

   b. Goal = Recovery (write "Recovery" on board and define using bullet points)

   - Recovery refers to a prosocial functioning at pre-illness levels and by desistence. Successful recovery will result in significant improvements in quality of life as CJ-PMI have increased good days, fewer hospital days and avoidance of re-incarceration.

3. **Distribute HANDOUT 1: Rules of the Pool**

   a. Have participants generate group rules. Facilitators ensure the following topics are included (write rules on the board):

   - Confidentiality—Define and explain the importance of confidentiality to the group members. Each participant will make a written and verbal commitment to the group that all discussions remain confidential.
   - Attendance—Participants are expected to attend all group activities. To successfully complete a module a participant may miss no more than two sessions for modules of 10 sessions or more in length, or one session for modules of eight or fewer sessions.
   - Promptness—Participants are expected to be on time for each and every group session. Tardiness distracts the

work of the group; thus, tardiness of greater than 10 minutes will be considered an absence, even if the individual attends the remainder of the group session (which is strongly encouraged—attend even if you are late and counted absent).

- Participation—Attendance is not sufficient. Remind participants they are expected to actively participate in group discussions.
- Respect—Each group member is expected to treat one another with respect. Challenges of behaviors, beliefs, and opinions are necessary for change to occur; however, all interactions and communications, including challenges, will be communicated respectfully. Group members do not have to like one another or agree with one another, but they must interact in a respectful manner.
- Homework—Inform participants that there are homework assignments for most sessions. Participants are responsible for completing *all* homework assignments by the beginning of the next group session.
- Rules to be determined by participants—Group participants are afforded an opportunity to develop additional rules that they believe are important for their group.

Note to therapists: the tardiness cutoff time should be developed with consideration of your institution. In some settings, it is not atypical that participants will be 10 or more minutes late for an appointment, but in other settings, 5 minutes might indicate significant and atypical tardiness.

---

b. Informed Consent

- Follow all policies and procedures for informed consent as governed by your institution, department, or agency.
- If the program is offered in a group format, at minimum obtain verbal consent from all participants to follow rules and maintain confidentiality (written consent is recommended).

4. **Introduce Preparation for Change Treatment Component**

a. Three sessions
b. To identify personal goals related to recovery
c. Participants are often ambivalent to change. This treatment module is designed to:

- Assess participant's readiness for change
- Enhance participant motivation to change.

d. In this treatment module, the participant will:

- Identify participant's life goals
- Quantify participant's life goals
- Outline benefits of participating in *Changing Lives for Changing Outcomes*.

5. **Complete WORKSHEET 1: Personal Problems**

a. If narrow, assist in expanding the scope of their problems.
b. Explore personal problems; classify them into personal and interpersonal.
c. These are the participant's self-perceived problems. Guidance may be necessary to assist with facilitation, but not with evaluation of problem areas.

6. **Complete Treatment Readiness Questionnaire**

a. Scoring:

- Reverse score items 1, 2, 3, 6, 13, 14, 16 and 19.
- Total scores = sum of all items (after recoding negatively keyed items).
- Subscale scores:
  - o Attitude and Motivation = sum items 1–6
  - o Emotional Reactions = sum items 7–12
  - o Offending Beliefs = sum items 12–16
  - o Efficacy = sum items 17–20.

b. Interpretation:

- Total scores range from 20 to 100. Higher scores are considered indicative of a higher degree of readiness to participate and engage in treatment (i.e., the higher the score the more treatment ready the individual). Subscale scores range from 6 to 30 (Attitude and Motivation and Emotional Reaction subscales) and 4 to 20 (Offending Beliefs and Efficacy subscales), with higher scores also representative of increased treatment readiness for the respective subscale.

7. **Assign HOMEWORK 1: Benefits of Change**

Session 2: Need for Intervention

Objective

This session will:
1. Build rapport with the participant
2. Help the participant understand the purpose for the intervention
3. Begin to examine the role of goals

The primary objective of the session is to introduce to the participant the need for them to define their own life goals and then introduce the idea that the program will show them how to get from here to there.

Materials

1. Blackboard or whiteboard (with chalk or markers) or flip chart (with markers)
2. HANDOUT 2: The Circle of Change
3. HANDOUT 3: Green Light to Recovery
4. WORKSHEET 2: Changing My Problem Areas
5. HANDOUT 4: Four Steps in Making Effective Goals
6. HOMEWORK 2: My Personal Goals

Session Content

1. **Collect and discuss HOMEWORK 1: Benefits of Change**

   a. Highlight universal benefits for group members (therapeutic factor of Universality) and hope for a better life with change (therapeutic factor of Installation of Hope).

2. **Review results from the Treatment Readiness Questionnaire**

   a. Integrate these results into discussion of how they need to accept responsibility for making changes in the areas discussed in Session 1 that have caused personal problems and problems for others.

3. **Provide overview of the program**

   a. Draw on the board the "You are here" and the "Your goals" circles and describe how the program is designed to fill in the steps to achieve your goals.

4. **Provide HANDOUT 2: The Circle of Change**
5. **Review HANDOUT 3: Green Light to Recovery**
6. **Complete WORKSHEET 2: Changing My Problem Areas**

   a. Provide non-judgmental feedback in small chunks.

7. **Discuss defining life goals. Write on the board: "What is a goal?"**

   a. Try to elicit the following response: a goal is something you want to achieve that is important to you—it is personal. You are responsible for achieving your goals. You may need resources and help from others, but you are accountable for whether you reach your goals.

8. **Write on the board: "Why are goals necessary/important?"**

   a. Try to elicit that they help you move in a certain direction, help you achieve what you want out of life, help you be more proud of yourself, and can help lead to larger goals.

9. Discuss steps in making effective goals. Write on the board: "What is an effective goal?"

    a. Try to elicit the following three components:

- Action: your goal should start with an "action" word
- Achievable: your goal must be realistic for you
- Results: you must be able to see the results and know when you have achieved your goal.

10. Distribute HANDOUT 4: Four Steps in Making Effective Goals, which describes the above components in greater detail

    a. Review the examples with the participants.

11. Assign HOMEWORK 2: My Personal Goals

    a. Inform participants they are now to generate four personal goals that fit the criteria of Action, Achievable, and Results.

    b. For participants' understanding, clinicians should distinguish between short- and long-term goals.

Session 3: Developing Our Goals

Objective

This session will:

1. Help the participant develop personal goals
2. Assist in identifying steps to achieving goals by identifying steps to achieve goals, resources available to help achieve goals, and sources of help.

The primary objective of this session is to reinforce the truism that words are easy (developing goals), and behavior change is the difficult part.

Materials

1. Blackboard or whiteboard (with chalk or markers) or flip chart (with markers)
2. HANDOUT 5: Steps, Resources, and Sources of Help
3. HOMEWORK 3: Developing Our Goals.

Session Content

1. Review HANDOUT 4: Four Steps in Making Effective Goals

2. Collect and review HOMEWORK 2: My Personal Goals. Have each participant offer an example and work to refine the goal statements as necessary

    a. Provide participants feedback on their goals and help clarify/specify goals as needed (take the necessary time to ensure that participants have specific, realistic, and achievable goals.

3. **Distribute HANDOUT 5: Steps, Resources, and Sources of Help**

    a. Now we are going to develop our goals further. Now that you have identified your goals, you have to:

        •   Identify the necessary steps to achieving your goal
        •   Identify your resources (what you have available to you now)
        •   Get help (identify what you don't have but need).

4. **Discuss HANDOUT 5: Steps, Resources, and Sources of Help,** explaining each step
5. Go back to one of the goals provided by a group member and walk through the steps using their goal as an example
6. Integrate and emphasize that health is necessary to accomplishing goals
7. **Assign HOMEWORK 3: Developing Our Goals**

14 Module II
Mental Illness and Criminalness Awareness

The aim of this treatment module is to facilitate CJ-PMI's understanding and recognition of their psychiatric symptomatology and criminal propensity that impacts their mental health and prosocial functioning. The principles guiding the "Mental Illness and Criminalness Awareness" treatment module are consistent with principles of psychosocial rehabilitation and the principles of Need and Responsivity from the Risk-Need-Responsivity model of corrections treatment. Consistent with the theoretical orientation of the *Changing Lives and Changing Outcomes* program, this module incorporates a social-cognitive learning theory with structured exercises (including in and outside of group exercises) to facilitate CJ-PMI awareness. By developing awareness of psychiatric symptomatology and their specific mental illness, as well as their criminal propensities, CJ-PMI will be better equipped to utilize subsequent modules aimed at behavioral change to facilitate improved outcomes, including reduced criminal and psychiatric recidivism (e.g., absence of imprisonment, fewer jail days, fewer hospital days, and improved psychosocial functioning—more good days).

Content

The "Mental Illness and Criminalness Awareness" module includes eight sessions to educate participants about mental illness, symptoms associated with mental illness, symptoms of criminalness, mechanisms for seeking help, and relapse prevention strategies.

Session 1 provides an overview of the module including outcome goals, a review of participant goals, and pre-testing.

Session 2 will educate participants about issues related to mental illness and the Recovery Model incorporated in this program.

Session 3 will educate participants about symptoms and issues specific to their mental illness.

Session 4 will challenge participants to accept responsibility for past choices they have made that limited their well-being, which blocked them from achieving their life goals, and challenge participants to accept responsibility for their future choices, recovery, and overall mental health functioning.

Session 5 will educate participants about symptoms and issues specific to their criminalness.

Session 6 will challenge participants to accept responsibility for past choices they have made that resulted in their legal problems, which blocked them from achieving their life goals, and challenge participants to accept responsibility for their future choices, recovery, and overall change in criminalness.

Session 7 will educate participants about the necessity of developing an effective relapse prevention plan and the mechanisms for developing this plan during the subsequent seven modules.

Session 8 will review participant's triggers for relapse and complete the module.

Treatment Process

As noted in *Changing Lives and Changing Outcomes*, all modules will be offered in a psychoeducational group setting. Although the theoretical orientation of the program integrates cognitive-behavioral and social-learning paradigms, the focus in this module is insight gained through education. That is, this module is unique from the other eight modules in that this module is content/learning driven. The goal of the "Mental Illness and Criminalness Awareness" module is knowledge accumulation and increased awareness of participant's mental illness and criminalness. Thus, the mechanism of change in this module is teaching based and didactic in nature. Similar to academic teaching, participants will be taught information and assigned tasks to facilitate their learning and retention of information for increased awareness. As the process for this module is psychoeducational in nature, each session is delivered with a cycle of content, in-class work, information handouts, and homework. Pre- and post-testing is conducted to measure both constructs and content of the group.

Treatment Goals

The overarching treatment goal of the "Mental Illness and Criminalness Awareness" module is the participant's insight. Specifically, this module aims to facilitate the participant's insight into their mental illness *and* their criminalness.

> *Insight into mental illness.* Insight is defined here as increased awareness and understanding of the participant's particular mental illness and the impact of this illness on their daily functioning.
> *Insight into criminalness.* Insight here is defined as understanding the areas of their lives that put them at risk for continued

antisocial behavior that violates social norms, the rights of others, and laws. Note that criminalness for purposes of this program is not limited to illegal behavior, rather it is defined as behavior that breaks laws and social conventions and/or violates the rights and well-being of others. We submit that participants engaging in any instance of non-prosocial behavior or decision making places them that much closer to repeating the criminal offense cycle; thus, insight here is aimed at helping participants identify all aspects of their antisocial decisions and behavior.

Session 1: An Introduction to Mental Illness and Criminalness Awareness

Objective

This session will:

1. Build rapport with the group
2. Introduce the program and educate participants about the importance of awareness of their mental illness and criminalness to their personal life goals
3. Complete pre-testing.

The primary objectives of the session are to provide participants an overview of the module including learning goals, review participant goals, revise participant goals as necessary, and complete pre-test measures.

Materials

1. Blackboard or whiteboard (with chalk or markers) or flip chart (with markers)
2. Pre-module Quiz
3. HOMEWORK 4: Recovery

Session Content

1. **Complete Pre-module Quiz**
2. **Welcome participants**

    a. Welcome and state name of treatment module.

3. **Review group rules (write rules on board and review verbally)**

    a. Same as from Module I: "Preparing for Change."

4. Introductions including mental health and criminal history (note: although this is redundant, group members are encouraged to be more open than they were in the first session (Module 1))

    a. Mental health history:

        • Diagnosis
        • Previous hospitalizations
        • Previous outpatient treatment
        • Current psychotropic medications.

Therapists Note: It is important to highlight commonalities during this exercise (Universality). It is important that group members connect with one another in terms of psychiatric history and mental health concerns, as well as criminal history and risk. This universality will greatly increase the functioning of the group as they support and challenge one another to change their behavior.

---

    b. Criminal history

        • Years in custody
        • Length of current sentence
        • Number of years of adult life in jail/prison
        • Types of offensive behavior not charged or convicted of

            o Include criminal behavior
            o Include non-criminal behavior.

5. **Provide an overview of the "Mental Illness and Criminalness Awareness" module**

    a. Explain format—total of eight sessions
    b. Goals:

        • Educate participants about mental illness
        • Educate participants about symptoms associated with mental illness
        • Educate participants about symptoms of criminalness
        • Educate participants about recognizing need and mechanisms for seeking help
        • Educate participants about importance of relapse prevention strategies.

6. **Define mental illness, criminalness, psychiatric recidivism, and criminal recidivism**

    a. Define verbally with explanation and write on blackboard:

        • Mental illness is a diagnosed psychiatric condition. It is analogous to cancer, diabetes, or any other diagnosis in that it is a genuine disorder that includes biological or physiological causes.

- Criminalness is a broader term than crime as it includes behaviors that may or may not break the law. For example, robbery and abuse of available sick time are both examples of criminalness. One breaks the law and one does not, but both include a general act of violating the rights and well-being of others with a general lack of responsible behavior.
- Psychiatric recidivism is the return of psychiatric clients to a psychiatric hospital. Anytime you are rehospitalized due to your mental illness, that is considered psychiatric recidivism.
- Criminal recidivism is the return of an individual to the criminal justice system (e.g., return to probation with a new charge, return to prison with a parole violation). Criminal recidivism can be the result of new charges or the result of a sanctioned failure (e.g., parole violation).

7. Review the life goals each participant developed in the Motivational Interviewing section

   a. Clarify any changes or revisions to their life goals.

8. **Discuss importance of participant's awareness (mental illness and criminalness) to their life goals**

   a. Questions:

      - What role does mental illness play in you ending up in custody or the hospital?
      - What role does your criminalness play in you ending up in custody or the hospital?
      - How does ending up in the hospital or custody impede your achieving your life goals?

9. **Assign HOMEWORK 4: Recovery**

Session 2: Recovery and Fact Finding

Objective

This session will:

1. Inquire about questions regarding Session 1
2. Educate participants about the Recovery Model
3. Educate participants about issues related to mental illness and criminalness.

The primary objective of this session is to educate participants about issues related to mental illness and the Recovery Model incorporated in this program.

Materials

1. Blackboard or whiteboard (with chalk or markers) or flip chart (with markers)
2. HANDOUT 6: Defining Recovery
3. HANDOUT 7: Facts About Mental Illness and Criminalness
4. HOMEWORK 5: What Is Mental Illness?

Session Content

1. **Review Session 1 and collect/review HOMEWORK 4: Recovery**
2. **Introduce "Recovery" as the goal of this treatment program**

   a. Refer to HANDOUT 6 (do not distribute at this point) to provide a definition of recovery.

3. **Define Recovery Model**

   a. Distribute HANDOUT 6: Defining Recovery
   b. Define the recovery model for the group
   c. Complete HANDOUT 6: Defining Recovery.

4. **Challenge negative thoughts/opposition to "recovery"**

   a. Ask for examples of messages they have received that oppose a Recovery Model (e.g., "You'll never get better," "You'll have to give up your goals," "You can't work/have children/ etc.," "You might as well give up on school/work," "Once a criminal, always a criminal," "You have a record, no one will hire you.")

   - Stigma is a particularly important issue to address.
   - Stigma will come up throughout the program if you are working in a group setting. These participant have a lot internalized stigma. Therapists may get resistance in the beginning talking about this; however, the more the participant trust the therapist, the more they are willing to talk about stigma. If you have group members that were never hospitalized you may see examples of stigma within the group setting (i.e., group members looking at other group members like they were crazy). This behavior is something to monitor and provides an excellent opportunity to process stigma in the here-and-now should it occur.

b. Explain these messages are discouraging and contribute to low expectations of themselves.

- Express empathy (e.g., "Sorry you were given that message")
- Focus on future and potential for change.

c. Challenge these messages

- Explore alternative ways of looking at the future
- Identify others that have overcome these messages.

5. **Educate participants about practical facts of mental illness and criminalness**

a. Distribute and Review HANDOUT 7: Facts about Mental Illness and Criminalness

6. **Teach the role of stress in mental illness and vulnerability to relapse**

a. More likely to experience exacerbation of symptoms
b. Harder to utilize coping strategies
c. Trigger indicating necessity of asking for help.

7. **Assign HOMEWORK 5: What Is Mental Illness?**

Session 3: What Is Mental Illness

Objective

This session will:

1. Educate participants about types of mental illnesses
2. Educate participants about symptoms of mental illness.

The primary objective of this session is to educate participants about symptoms and issues specific to their mental illness.

Materials

1. Blackboard or whiteboard (with chalk or markers) or flip chart (with markers)
2. HANDOUT 8: Practical Facts About Depression
3. HANDOUT 9: Practical Facts About Bipolar Disorder
4. HANDOUT 10: Practical Facts About Schizophrenia
5. HOMEWORK 6a and 6b: What Is My Illness and What Are My Symptoms

Session Content

1. Ask for questions regarding Session 2 or HOMEWORK 5: What Is Mental Illness?
2. Collect homework and briefly review content of Session 2
3. What is depression?

    a. Distribute HANDOUT 8: Practical Facts About Depression
    b. Review handout and seek feedback from participants about their experiences

    •   e.g., symptoms they've experienced.

4. What is bipolar disorder?

    a. Distribute HANDOUT 9: Practical Facts About Bipolar Disorder
    b. Review handout and seek feedback from participants about their experiences

    •   e.g., symptoms they've experienced.

5. What is schizophrenia?

    a. Distribute HANDOUT 10: Practical Facts About Schizophrenia
    b. Review handout and seek feedback from participants about their experiences

    •   e.g., symptoms they've experienced.

6. **Review HOMEWORK 5: What Is Mental Illness? and correct erroneous answers**
7. Identify key learning points from Session 3

    a. Participants should identify key learning points (points they found interesting and beneficial)
    b. Have participants identify three primary symptoms of their mental illness (symptoms they experience).

8. **Assign HOMEWORK 6a and 6b: What Is My Illness and What Are My Symptoms**

    (Homework designed to help participants identify specifics of their illness.)

Session 4: What Is My Mental Illness

Objective

This session will:

1. Educate participants about the impact of mental illness on their life choices

2. Challenge participants to accept responsibility for their recovery and mental health functioning.

The primary objective of this session is to challenge participants to accept responsibility for past choices they have made that limited their well-being, which blocked them from achieving their life goals, and challenge participants to accept responsibility for their future choices, recovery, and overall mental health functioning.

Materials

1. Blackboard or whiteboard (with chalk or markers) or flip chart (with markers)
2. QUIZ 1: Questions About Mental Illness
3. HANDOUT 11: Stigma and Coping With Mental Illness
4. HOMEWORK 7: Coping With My Mental Illness

Session Content

1. **Administer QUIZ 1: Questions About Mental Illness**
2. **Review answers for QUIZ 1: Questions About Mental Illness**

    a. Grade aloud and correct erroneous answers.

3. **Review content from Session 3**
4. **Ask for questions regarding Session 3 and review HOMEWORK 6a and 6b: What Is My Illness and What Are My Symptoms**
5. **Discuss with participants the relationship between some of their problems and symptoms of their mental illness**

    a. Have participants identify chronic problems they have:

    - Examples

        o   Lack of energy
        o   Distractibility
        o   Poor motivation/initiation
        o   Too much or too little sleep
        o   Poor work/school performance
        o   Fuzzy memory
        o   Odd/eccentric behavior.

    b. Help participants identify how these problems are related to their mental illness

    - Mental illness is not an excuse, rather an explanation for why they feel or think the way they do.
    - Participants remain responsible for their mental health functioning and for coping effectively even when experiencing negative symptoms.

6. Define stigma (see **HANDOUT 11: Stigma and Coping With Mental Illness)**

7. Distribute **HANDOUT 11: Stigma and Coping With Mental Illness**

   a. Help participants identify effective coping strategies for managing their symptoms/mental illness.

8. Assign **HOMEWORK 7: Coping With My Mental Illness**

Quiz 1: Questions About Mental Illness

1. Which of these is not a mental illness?

    a.   Depression
    b.   Violence (c)
    c.   Bipolar disorder
    d.   Schizophrenia

2. Which of these is not a symptom of schizophrenia?

    a.   Hallucinations
    b.   Violence (c)
    c.   Delusions
    d.   Problems with friends and work

3. Depression is:

    a.   A very rarely diagnosed mental illness
    b.   An uncommon mental illness
    c.   A common mental illness
    d.   The most common mental illness (c)

4. Symptoms of most mental illnesses develop in

    a.   Childhood
    b.   Young adulthood (c)
    c.   Late adulthood
    d.   The elderly

5. Which of these symptoms is unique to bipolar disorder?

    a.   Excessive spending (c)
    b.   Suicidal thoughts
    c.   Sad mood
    d.   Hallucinations

6. Psychotic symptoms are:

    a.   A group of symptoms that make people look sad
    b.   A group of symptoms that make people look happy
    c.   A group of symptoms that makes people believe imagined things are real (c)
    d.   A group of symptoms that makes people look angry

7. Which of these is not a symptom of depression?

    a. Sad mood
    b. Exercising a lot (c)
    c. Suicidal thoughts
    d. Eating a lot

8. Mental illnesses are diagnosed by:

    a. Mental health professionals
    b. Doctors
    c. Correctional officers
    d. Both A and B (c)
    e. All of the above

9. Treatment for mental illness is:

    a. Not available but would be effective
    b. Effective and available (c)
    c. Available but not effective
    d. Not worth worrying about

10. Which one of these famous people does/did not have a mental illness?

    a. Beyoncé (c)
    b. Terry Bradshaw
    c. Jim Carrey
    d. Abraham Lincoln

11. Someone with a mental illness has won a Nobel Prize.

    a. True (c)
    b. False

12. What is stigma?

    a. An eye condition
    b. A positive opinion about a group of people that someone knows a lot about
    c. A positive opinion about a group of people that someone knows nothing about
    d. A negative opinion about a group of people that someone knows nothing about (c)

13. It is illegal not to hire someone who is mentally ill on the basis that they are mentally ill.

   a. True (c)
   b. False

14. Which of these are strategies that someone can use to help respond to stigma?

   a. Learn about mental disorders
   b. Sleep until you feel better
   c. Eat until you feel better
   d. Become aware of your legal rights
   e. A and D only (c)
   f. All of the above

15. How can someone help manage their mental illness?

   a. Build a social support network
   b. Develop a relapse prevention plan
   c. Learn how to cope with symptoms
   d. B and C only
   e. All of the above (c)

16. Once you have a mental illness, you:

   a. Have a brain disease
   b. Will never be healthy again
   c. Can lead a normal life (c)
   d. Are destined to spend time in jail

17. The biggest barrier to mental illness recovery is:

   a. The attitude of the general population (c)
   b. Doctors not prescribing enough medication
   c. No research on mental illness
   d. Non-supportive friends and family

18. Which of these things can be helpful in recovery?

   a. Art
   b. Exercise
   c. Learning to control symptoms
   d. All of the above (c)

19. Compared to other diseases, mental illness can be treated:

    a. Easier
    b. Harder
    c. About the same (c)
    d. Mental illness is not like other diseases

20. People who have mental illness are:

    a. Violent
    b. Crazy
    c. People who should not be in public
    d. All of the above
    e. None of the above (c)

21. Mental illness can affect:

    a. Children
    b. Adults
    c. The elderly
    d. All of the above (c)
    e. B and C only

22. Which of these things will help you stay well when you have a mental condition?

    a. Connecting with others
    b. Advocating for yourself
    c. Getting the care you need
    d. Planning a sleep schedule
    e. Watching what you eat
    f. Managing stress
    g. Exercising
    h. Doing something you enjoy
    i. All of the above (c)

23. Schizophrenia is:

    a. A disorder that causes split personalities
    b. A disorder that makes it hard to distinguish real and fake (c)
    c. A disease caused by poor parenting
    d. A disease that only affects unlucky people

24. Depression is:

    a. A disease that is characterized by sad moods and fatigue (c)
    b. A disease that is characterized by hyper moods and excessive spending
    c. A disease that is characterized by a lack of emotion
    d. A disease that lies dormant in the body until a person gets older

25. Bipolar disorder is categorized as:

    a. A disorder that can have really high moods
    b. A disorder that can have really low moods
    c. A disorder that is characterized by a really flat mood
    d. Both A and B (c)

26. Schizophrenia is caused by:

    a. Excessive alcohol and drug use
    b. A person's genetics
    c. A person's stress level
    d. All of the above
    e. B and C only (c)

27. Depression, schizophrenia, and bipolar disorder:

    a. Always have the same symptoms in each person
    b. Are very unique from one another
    c. Share many of the same symptoms (c)
    d. Have nothing in common with one another

Session 5: What Is Criminalness

Objective

This session will:

1. Educate participants about factors contributing to criminalness
2. Educate participants about symptoms of criminalness.

The primary objective of the session is to educate participants about symptoms and issues specific to their criminalness. Note that it is our experience that both therapists and participant particularly enjoy this session. Although CJ-PMI are initially resistant to the term "criminalness," once explained, you will likely find that they quickly adopt this phrase as a common part of their everyday vocabulary.

Materials

1. Blackboard or whiteboard (with chalk or markers) or flip chart (with markers)
2. HANDOUT 12: Practical Facts About Crime and Criminalness
3. HANDOUT 13: Symptoms of Criminalness
4. HOMEWORK 8: My Symptoms of Criminalness

Session Content

1. **Ask for questions regarding Session 4 or HOMEWORK 7: Coping With My Mental Illness**
2. **Collect homework and briefly review content of Session 4**
3. **What is criminalness?**

   a. Provide a brief verbal definition of criminalness—criminalness is not limited to illegal behavior, rather it is defined as behavior that breaks laws and social conventions and/or violates the rights and well-being of others.

Therapist Note: therapists need to be prepared for participants to be very defensive and potentially argumentative about their status as "criminals." They may feel insulted, offended, and believe that you are calling them a bad person. In the beginning, they equate "criminal" with a bad person. They will voice how they are not bad people, just people who made bad choices. It is your task to educate them that criminalness is not a label, rather a way of identifying behaviors that contribute to irresponsible behavior, and that supports criminal and non-criminal behaviors (i.e., any behaviors that are not prosocial in nature).

4. **Distribute HANDOUT 12: Practical Facts About Crime and Criminalness**

   a. What is crime?
   b. Explain criminalness
   c. Discuss recidivism and criminal risk factors

   - Explain and define criminal thinking and attitudes

     o Review examples of criminal thinking and attitudes

   - Explain criminal associates

     o Obtain examples of criminal associates in participants' lives

   - Explain substance abuse and relationship to criminalness

     o Discuss participants' substance use. Include substance use connected to criminal acts rather caught or not caught (e.g., obtaining/using illicit substances, committing crime while intoxicated, driving while intoxicated)

   d. Explain work and leisure and relationship to crime
   e. Explain family and marital functioning and relationship to crime
   f. Explain mental health functioning and relationship to crime.

5. **What are symptoms of criminalness?**

   a. Distribute HANDOUT 13: Symptoms of Criminalness

   - Discuss common symptoms of criminalness

     o e.g., boredom, anger/frustration with current lot in life, financial difficulties, mental illness symptoms, emotions management, other symptoms you observed with your participants or from your experience

   - Help participants identify how these problems are related to their criminalness
   - These symptoms are not an excuse, rather an explanation for why they feel or think the way they do
   - Participants remain responsible for prosocial (responsible) behavior and their overall functioning and for coping effectively with these problems/symptoms and desisting from crime
   - Define and explain "desistence."

6. **Identify key learning points from Session 5**

   a. Participants should identify key learning points (points they found interesting and beneficial)
   b. Have participants identify three primary symptoms of their criminalness (symptoms they experience).

7. **Assign HOMEWORK 8: My Symptoms of Criminalness**

Session 6: What Is My Criminalness

Objective

This session will:

1. Educate participants about the impact of criminalness on their life choices and subsequent consequences
2. Challenge participants to accept responsibility for their recovery and changing their criminalness.

The primary objective of the session is to challenge participants to accept responsibility for past choices they have made that resulted in their legal problems, which blocked them from achieving their life goals, and challenge participants to accept responsibility for their future choices, recovery, and overall change in criminalness.

Materials

1. Blackboard or whiteboard (with chalk or markers) or flip chart (with markers)
2. HANDOUT 14: My Criminalness
3. HOMEWORK 9: Pervasiveness and Coping With My Criminalness

Session Content

1. **Ask for questions regarding Session 5 and review HOMEWORK 8: My Symptoms of Criminalness**
2. **Distribute HANDOUT 14: My Criminalness**
3. **Ask participants to compare their responses to HOMEWORK 8: My Symptoms of Criminalness and HANDOUT 14: My Criminalness**

   a. Encourage participants to recognize their limited insight into criminalness, including antecedents to criminal behavior

      • Define and explain "antecedents" (the situation, events or circumstances that precede a criminal act and likely serve as triggers) and explain in relation to criminal acts
      • Summarize criminalness as a general lack of responsibility and that a life without responsible living is analogous to an alcoholic refusing to abstain from alcohol.

4. **Discuss with participants the relationship between some of their symptoms (problems) and their criminalness**

a. Have participants identify chronic problems they have:

- Examples
    - o Lack of energy
    - o Distractibility
    - o Poor motivation/initiation
    - o Too much or too little sleep
    - o Poor work/school performance
    - o Fuzzy memory
    - o Odd/eccentric behavior.

b. Help participants identify how these problems are related to their mental illness

- Mental illness is not an excuse, rather an explanation for why they feel or think the way they do.
- Participants remain responsible for their mental health functioning and for coping effectively even when experiencing negative symptoms.

c. Help participants identify effective coping strategies for managing their symptoms/mental illness

5. **Assign HOMEWORK 9: Pervasiveness and Coping With My Criminalness**

Session 7: Relapse Prevention for My Mental Illness and Criminalness

Objective

This session will:

1. Educate participants about relapse prevention and the role it plays in effective management of mental illness and criminalness
2. Educate participants about effective components of an effective relapse prevention plan
3. Educate participants about the remaining seven treatment modules and how they will develop a relapse prevention plan for recovery that integrates their problems with mental illness and criminalness

The primary objective of the session is to educate participants about the necessity of developing an effective relapse prevention plan and the mechanisms for developing this plan during the next seven modules.

Materials

1. Blackboard or whiteboard (with chalk or markers) or flip chart (with markers)
2. HANDOUT 15: Signs and Symptoms of Relapse
3. WORKSHEET 3: Effective Components of a Relapse Prevention Plan
4. HOMEWORK 10: My Triggers

Session Content

1. **Ask for questions regarding Session 6 and review HOMEWORK 9: Pervasiveness and Coping With My Criminalness**

   a. Remind participants that criminalness is not simply about the crimes they are convicted of, but all the behaviors (criminal and non-criminal) that show a general lack of responsibility and violate the rights and well-being of others.

2. **Review content of Sessions 1–6**

   a. Specific content to review:

      • Recovery
      • Facts about mental illness and criminalness
      • Specific type of mental illness discussed (schizophrenia, bipolar disorder, and depression)
      • Symptoms of mental illness
      • Facts about criminalness
      • Symptoms of criminalness.

3. **Define and explain relapse**

   a. Distribute and review HANDOUT 15: Signs and Symptoms of Relapse

      • Define "triggers" (red light) and early warning signs (yellow light) and the role of each in relapse.

4. **Explain components of an effective relapse plan**

   a. Distribute and review WORKSHEET 3: Effective Components of a Relapse Plan
   b. Explain how the relapse plan will be developed during each of the remaining modules.

5. **Assign HOMEWORK 10: My Triggers**

Session 8: Concluding Mental Illness and Criminalness Awareness

Objective

This session will:

1. Review participant's identification of triggers to mental illness and criminalness relapse
2. Highlight participant's strengths and learning during the program
3. Distribute "Mental Illness and Criminalness Awareness" graduation certificates
4. Complete module post-testing

The primary objective of the session is to review participant's triggers for relapse, award graduate certificates, and complete post-test measures.

Materials

1. Blackboard or whiteboard (with chalk or markers) or flip chart (with markers)
2. "Mental Illness and Criminalness Awareness" graduation certificates
3. Post-module Quiz

Session Content

1. **Ask for questions regarding Session 7 and review HOMEWORK 10: My Triggers**

    a. Remind participants that they will develop specific relapse plans during the course of the next seven modules.

2. **Reinforce group participation**

    a. Highlight:

    • Group participants' strengths
    • Group participants' learning during the program
    • And reinforce group participants' active participation and completion of homework assignments

    b. As noted by one therapist during field testing:

    So important! I think this had a huge impact, in fact one group member thanked me for doing it. They don't often get praised. It was a good self-esteem booster, Instillation of Hope. Additionally, I was reminded of the Altruism Factor. It is important as they move through the group to point out how useful and helpful some group members have been to others. This helped my guys, particularly because they abuse alcohol and illicit substances, feel useful to others.

3. Distribute "Mental Illness and Criminalness Awareness" graduation certificates.
4. Complete Post-module Quiz

15 Module III
Thoughts and Attitudes

This module includes 13 therapeutic sessions designed to facilitate a process of learning to identify, evaluate, and modify thinking and cognitive attitudes that contribute to criminalness and perpetuate impaired mental health functioning. CJ-PMI think differently than non-CJ-PMI, and the premise for this module is that *the way people think affects their behavior* (i.e., how people think affects how they act). In other words, it is the way a person construes (thinks about) a situation that influences their feelings and behaviors. Thus, the foundation for this treatment component is a cognitive model that applies to a CJ-PMI population as thinking styles and attitudes are common to criminal behavior, as well as impaired mental health functioning. Specifically, cognitive restructuring (cognitive-behavioral techniques for altering one's thoughts) will be used to facilitate changes in thoughts and beliefs that increase risk for criminal behavior, as well as thoughts and beliefs that contribute to negative feelings and dysfunctional behavior.

Content

The "Thoughts and Attitudes" module includes 13 sessions to educate participants about different types of thinking styles (referred to as criminal thinking) that support their involvement in crime and interfere with their mental health recovery, and to utilize cognitive-behavioral strategies (e.g., charting, cognitive restructuring) to modify these thinking styles.

Session 1 includes a pre-test quiz, reviewing the group rules, and reviewing participants' personal goals. The session will also introduce the "Thoughts and Attitudes" module and teach participants the relationship between thoughts, feelings, and behavior.

Session 2 reviews the relationship between thoughts, feelings, and behavior, and teaches participants the eight criminal thinking errors of focus in this program.

Session 3 will continue to teach participants about criminal thinking and help them identify criminal thinking as it occurs in others (via a movie).

Session 4 will continue to teach participants about automatic thoughts and help them identify their automatic thoughts via the movie begun in Session 3.

Session 5 will educate participants on the connection between their automatic thoughts and criminal behavior, and introduce them to the eight types of criminal thinking utilized in this treatment program. Finally, participants will receive their PICTS assessment scores from their pre-test assessments.

Session 6 will continue to educate participants about criminal thinking, teach participants about automatic thoughts and what automatic thoughts are, and teach participants the relationship between automatic thoughts, feelings, and subsequent behavior.

Session 7 will continue educating participants about the effect of automatic thoughts on behavior (including behavior related to criminalness and mental illness). This session will also continue teaching participants how to monitor their automatic thoughts.

Session 8 will review participants' progress with regard to self-monitoring automatic thoughts. The session will also continue to provide feedback to participants to improve recording behavior (Automatic Thought Log), and begin to teach participants how to challenge their automatic thoughts.

Sessions 9–12 will continue educating participants about the effect of automatic thoughts on behavior (including behavior related to criminalness and mental illness), continue teaching participants how to monitor their automatic thoughts, and continue teaching participants how to challenge their automatic thoughts.

Session 13 will continue to review participants' recognition of their automatic thoughts and the connection between these thoughts and their criminal behavior and mental health functioning. This session will then focus on relapse planning regarding antisocial cognitions and attitudes, and will conclude with the module post-test.

Treatment Process

The "Thoughts and Attitudes" module is grounded in traditional cognitive-behavioral theory with emphasis on participants learning to recognize automatic thoughts that contribute to criminal behavior and poorer mental health functioning. Emphasis is placed on cognitive restructuring whereby participants learn to change their automatic thoughts. Social-learning paradigms are relevant to this module. Consistent with the *CLCO* program, this module integrates a psychoeducational format with structured learning activities to include in-class work, informational handouts, and homework. Specifically, psychoeducational exercises will be implemented to teach criminal thinking errors to members and to help them identify the thinking errors that permeate their thoughts. Cognitive restructuring will be used in this module to help participants begin to modify their thinking errors.

Treatment Goals

The overarching treatment goals of the "Thoughts and Attitudes" module are that participants will:

1. Understand the relationship between thoughts, feelings, and behavior
2. Understand automatic thoughts
3. Learn to monitor and challenge their automatic thoughts.

Session 1: Thoughts and Attitudes

Objective

This session will:

1. Complete pre-testing
2. Review group rules
3. Review participant's personal goals
4. Introduce the "Thoughts and Attitudes" module.

The primary objective of this session is to teach participants the relationship between thoughts, feelings, and subsequent behavior.

Materials

1. Blackboard or whiteboard (with chalk or markers) or flip chart (with markers)
2. Pre-module Quiz

Session Content

1. **Complete Pre-module Quiz**
2. **Review group rules (write rules on board and review verbally—optional)**

    a. HANDOUT 1: Rules of the Pool

3. **Review participant's personal goals (see HOMEWORK 2 from "Preparing for Change" module)**

    a. Each participant reviews their personal goals aloud to the group.

4. Teach participants about thoughts, feelings, and behavior (traditional ABC model) using the Circle of Change (see HANDOUT 2 from the "Preparing for Change" module)

   a. Teach participants about purposeful thought vs. automatic thoughts

      • Automatic thoughts are thoughts that pop into our head in response to stimuli or situations
      • They are automatic in that they are spontaneous and not intentional thoughts
      • Give examples:

         o Two people walking down the street and accidently bump shoulders—some might automatically think it was purposeful (e.g., a power move) without using purposeful thought to assess the situation
         o Get a failing grade on a GED test—some might think "I'm stupid" without using purposeful thought to assess prior successes and totality of one's ability
         o Ask for examples from their lives.

   b. Teach participants how thoughts affect feelings.
   c. Teach participations how thoughts and feelings affect behavior.

Session 2: Criminal Thinking

Objective

This session will:

1. Review homework
2. Review relationship between thoughts, feelings, and subsequent behavior
3. Discuss positive cognitive processes
4. Teach participants about the criminal thinking errors used in this program.

The primary objective of this session is to teach participants the eight types of criminal thinking errors.

Materials

1. Blackboard or whiteboard (with chalk or markers) or flip chart (with markers)
2. HANDOUT 16: Common Errors of Criminal Thinking
3. HOMEWORK 11: Examples of My Criminal Thinking

Session Content

1. **Review Session 1**

    a. Reinforce participants' recognition of their criminal thinking
    b. Review the outcomes, highlighting negative outcomes that result from criminal thinking.

2. **Teach participants about criminal thinking**

    a. CJ-PMI think differently than non-CJ-PMI
    b. Distribute HANDOUT 16: Common Errors of Criminal Thinking

    - Review what criminal thinking is and is not

        o *Is* a process of thinking supportive of crime
        o *Is not* thoughts about specific criminal acts.

Therapist Note: Many participant will get bogged down trying to memorize the actual names of the eight criminal thinking errors, so it may be beneficial here to emphasize that, at this stage, it is important for them to know all eight concepts, but not necessarily the name of each thinking error.

    - Review the types of criminal thinking
    - Review participants PICTS-SF and MCAA (Part II) scores from program pretesting (PICTS-SF and MCAA handouts from Module II)
    - Ask participants for examples of how the three types of criminal thinking "fit" for them

        o Write those examples on the handout.

3. **Assign HOMEWORK 11: Examples of My Criminal Thinking**

Session 3: Identifying Criminal Thinking

Objective

This session will:

1. Continue to teach participants about criminal thinking and help them identify criminal thinking as it occurs in others (via a movie).

The primary objective of this session is to continue educating participants about the presence of criminal thinking and the effect of criminal thinking in their lives.

Materials

1. Blackboard or whiteboard (with chalk or markers) or flip chart (with markers)
2. Movie of choice (recommendations below)
3. WORKSHEET 4: Identifying Criminal Thinking

Session Content

1. **Review Session 2 and review HOMEWORK 11: Examples of My Criminal Thinking**

   a. Reinforce participants' recognition of their criminal thinking
   b. Review the outcomes, highlighting negative outcomes that result from criminal thinking.

2. **Show movie that includes examples of mental illness and criminal thinking**

   a. Movies that are entertaining, but also show the interaction of mental illness and criminalness are particularly beneficial

      • Examples:

         o Silver Linings Playbook
         o Girl, Interrupted
         o One Flew Over the Cuckoo's Nest
         o The Amazing Spiderman (2012, 2014).

   b. Provide WORKSHEET 4: Identifying Criminal Thinking

      • Pause movie frequently to allow participants time to write and discuss.

Therapist Note: You will have two sessions to watch and review this movie, so frequent starting and stopping to allow for discussion is strongly encouraged.

---

3. **Discuss and review WORKSHEET 4: Identifying Criminal Thinking (time permitting)**

   a. Ask participants what they learned from this exercise
   b. Inform participants to bring the handout to the next session as you will continue your discussion and the movie.

Session 4: More Identifying Criminal Thinking

Objective

This session will:

1. Continue to teach participants about automatic thoughts and help them identify their automatic thoughts via the movie begun in Session 3.

The primary objective of this session is to continue educating participants about the presence of criminal thinking and the effect of criminal thinking in their lives.

Materials

1. Blackboard or whiteboard (with chalk or markers) or flip chart (with markers)
2. Movie of choice
3. HOMEWORK 12: More Examples of My Criminal Thinking

Session Content

1. **Review Session 3**

   a. Review plot of movie and instances of criminal thinking
   b. Reinforce participants' recognition of their criminal thinking
   c. Review the outcomes in the movie with emphasis on highlighting negative outcomes that result from criminal thinking.

2. **Continue the movie from Session 3**
3. **Continue WORKSHEET 4: Identifying Criminal Thinking (time permitting)**
4. **Assign HOMEWORK 12: More Examples of My Criminal Thinking**

Session 5: Criminal Thinking and Automatic Thoughts

Objective

This session will:

1. Teach participants about automatic thoughts (what automatic thoughts are and are not)
2. Show participants their criminal thinking.

The primary objective of this session is to educate participants about automatic thoughts, including the impact of automatic thoughts on behavior. This session will also educate participants about eight types of criminal thinking and provide them data on their criminal thinking (from their pre-assessment).

Materials

1. Blackboard or whiteboard (with chalk or markers) or flip chart (with markers)
2. HANDOUT 17: Automatic Thoughts
3. Pre-test PICTS Scores and Graphs for each participant
4. HOMEWORK 12: More Examples of My Criminal Thinking

Session Content

1. **Teach participants about automatic thoughts and how they lead to criminal thinking**

    a. Distribute HANDOUT 17: Automatic Thoughts

        • Review what criminal thinking is and is not

            o   *Is* a process of thinking supportive of crime
            o   *Is not* thoughts about specific criminal acts.

        • Review eight types of criminal thinking
        • Ask participants which of the three types of criminal thinking "fit" for them

            o   Write those that "fit" on the handout.

    b. Review participants PICTS and MCAA Part II scores from program pre-assessment

        • Review HANDOUT 14: My Criminalness to review eight PICTS scale scores and MCAA attitude scores
        • Compare elevated scale scores with those they thought "fit" for them (HANDOUT 16: Common Errors of Criminal Thinking)
        • Ask for examples of how their criminal thinking impacts their behavior

            o   Focus on negative outcomes resulting from these examples.

2. **Re-assign HOMEWORK 12: More Examples of My Criminal Thinking**

Session 6: Thoughts Lead to Feelings, Which Leads to Behavior

Objective

This session will:

1. Continue educating participants about criminal thinking
2. Teach participants about automatic thoughts and what automatic thoughts are
3. Teach participants the relationship between automatic thoughts, feelings, and subsequent behavior.

The primary objectives of this session are to reinforce participants' understanding of criminal thinking and the effect of criminal thinking in their lives. This session will also teach participants about the relationship between automatic thoughts, feelings, and their behavior.

Materials

1. Blackboard or whiteboard (with chalk or markers) or flip chart (with markers)
2. HOMEWORK 13: My Criminal Thinking and Automatic Thoughts

Session Content

1. **Discuss and review WORKSHEET 4: Identifying Criminal Thinking (handout was completed in Session 2 of this module)**

   a. Help participants recognize examples of criminal thinking in different characters of the movie
   b. Reinforce negative outcomes that occur as a result of criminal thinking
   c. Highlight interaction of criminalness and mental illness in association with criminal thinking.

2. **Continue to teach participants about automatic thoughts**

   a. Review HANDOUT 17: Automatic Thoughts from previous session

      • Focus on relationship between automatic thoughts, feelings, and subsequent behavior (use flow chart in handout)

         o Provide examples (minimum of three)

            a. Draw examples on board using the flow chart from HANDOUT 17
            b. Possible examples (or use your own)

      i. Example 1: Event = Police officer pulls you over for speeding

     ii. Example 2: Event = Your doctor is not responding to your complaints of negative side effects

    iii. Example 3: Event = Probation officer gives you more than the usual number of urinary analysis and home visits.

3. **Assign HOMEWORK 13: My Criminal Thinking and Automatic Thoughts**

    a. Provide multiple copies so participants do not limit their logging of automatic thoughts prior to the next session.

Session 7: Better Recognizing Automatic Thoughts

Objective

This session will:

1. Continue educating participants about the effect of automatic thoughts on behavior (including behavior related to criminalness and mental illness)
2. Continue teaching participants how to monitor their automatic thoughts.

The primary objectives of this session are to ensure that participants effectively monitor their automatic thoughts and related criminal thinking. No new information is presented in this session, so participants can work on "overlearning" this information.

Materials

1. Blackboard or whiteboard (with chalk or markers) or flip chart (with markers)
2. Blank typing paper (minimum of two pages per participant)
3. HOMEWORK 13: My Criminal Thinking and Automatic Thoughts

Session Content

1. **Ask for questions regarding Session 6 or HOMEWORK 13: My Criminal Thinking and Automatic Thoughts**
2. **Review HOMEWORK 13: My Criminal Thinking and Automatic Thoughts**

    a. Reinforce efforts to complete the homework

- Inform participants that effectively monitoring their thinking is a skill

  - o   As with any skill, it takes time to develop the skill (e.g., riding a bike took time to learn).

b.   Provide feedback to participants that did not complete the homework or were not effective in their record keeping

c.   Facilitate a group discussion focusing on how the thoughts identified in their automatic thought logs led to problematic behaviors

- Emphasize effect on efforts toward recovery (long-term goals).

d.   Reinforce potential for change to improve probability of recovery.

3.   **Instruct participants to select one entry from the Automatic Thought Log and to graph the chain of events (flow chart as presented in Session 6)**

a.   Any participant that did not complete the homework should be provided an example from another participant's completed homework

b.   Discuss the chain of events and highlight point of intervention (stoplight point from HANDOUT 17: Automatic Thoughts)

c.   Repeat this exercise (three times total if time permits)

- Upon second and third graph, instruct participants to identify at what point they needed to assume responsibility for the situation (including their thoughts, feelings, and behaviors) and how they recognized the point to intervene (trigger).

4.   **Re-assign HOMEWORK 13: My Criminal Thinking and Automatic Thoughts**

a.   Provide multiple copies so participants do not limit their logging of automatic thoughts prior to the next session.

Session 8: Red Light—Challenging Automatic Thoughts

Objective

This session will:

1.   Review participants' progress with regard to self-monitoring automatic thoughts by continuing to provide feedback to participants to improve recording behavior (Automatic Thought Log)
2.   Begin to teach participants how to challenge their automatic thoughts.

The primary objectives of this session are to help participants continue to effectively monitor their automatic thoughts and related criminal thinking. This session will also present participants with a strategy for challenging their automatic thoughts.

Materials

1. Blackboard or whiteboard (with chalk or markers) or flip chart (with markers)
2. Blank index/recipe cards
3. HANDOUT 18: Challenging My Automatic Thoughts
4. HOMEWORK 14: Challenging Automatic Thoughts Log

Session Content

1. **Ask for questions regarding Session 7**
2. **Review HOMEWORK 13: My Criminal Thinking and Automatic Thoughts**

   a. Again reinforce efforts to complete the homework

      - Inform participants that effectively monitoring their thinking is a skill

        o As with any skill, it takes time to develop the skill (e.g., riding a bike took time to learn).

   b. Continue to provide feedback to participants that did not complete the homework or were not effective in their record keeping
   c. Facilitate a group discussion focusing on how the thoughts identified in their automatic thought logs led to problematic behaviors

      - Emphasize effect on efforts toward recovery (long-term goals).

   d. Reinforce potential for change to improve probability of recovery.

3. **Teach participants how to challenge their automatic thoughts**

   a. Distribute and review HANDOUT 18: Challenging My Automatic Thoughts

---

Note to Therapists: You should attempt to make these six questions as simple as possible for the participants to understand. The questions they write on their index/recipe cards should be as simple as possible and in their own words.

---

b. Select examples from HOMEWORK 13 (the reassignment of HOMEWORK 13) and help the group work through situations with the six questions incorporated to challenge the listed automatic thoughts

- Use as many examples as time permits.

4. Explain that participants need to use these questions to challenge their automatic thoughts in their everyday lives

   a. To facilitate participants' memory of the six questions, they should write the questions down on a 3x5 index card that can be easily and discreetly carried around with them throughout the day. This card is referred to as a Cue Card.

5. Assign HOMEWORK 14: Challenging Automatic Thoughts Log

   a. Complete the first row with participants by using an example from HOMEWORK 13

6. Also assign participants to carry their Que Card with them everywhere they go for the remainder of this module

   a. Check on this assignment in each of the remaining five sessions of this module

Session 9: Less Red Light—Changing Automatic Thoughts

Objective

This session will:

1. Continue educating participants about the effect of automatic thoughts on behavior (including behavior related to criminalness and mental illness)
2. Continue teaching participants how to monitor their automatic thoughts
3. Continue teaching participants how to challenge their automatic thoughts.

The primary objective of this session is to ensure that participants continue to challenge their automatic thoughts and related criminal thinking. No new information is presented in this session, so participants can work on "overlearning" this information.

Materials

1. Blackboard or whiteboard (with chalk or markers) or flip chart (with markers)
2. Blank typing paper (minimum of two pages per participant)
3. HOMEWORK 14: Challenging Automatic Thoughts Log

Session Content

1. **Ask for questions regarding Session 8 or HOMEWORK 14: Challenging Automatic Thoughts Log**
2. **Review HOMEWORK 14: Challenging Automatic Thoughts Log**

   a.   Reinforce efforts to complete the homework

      • Inform participants that effectively challenging their thinking is a skill (just like learning to monitor their thinking in previous sessions of this module)

         o   As with any skill, it takes time to develop the skill (e.g., riding a bike took time to learn).

   b.   Provide feedback to participants that did not complete the homework or were not effective in their record keeping

      • Discuss barriers to completing homework and develop a plan for working around those barriers.

   c.   Facilitate a group discussion on the difficulty and effectiveness of challenging their automatic thoughts

      • Emphasize the effect on efforts toward recovery (long-term goals).

   d.   Reinforce potential for change to improve probability of recovery.

3. **Instruct participants to select one entry from one participants Challenging Automatic Thoughts Log and graph the chain of events (flow chart as presented in Session 6)**

   a.   Use the board or flip chart to graph the chain of events for all to see

      • Participants should also graph the chain of events on blank pieces of white typing paper

   b.   Any participant that did not complete the homework should be provided an example from another participant's completed homework

   c.   Discuss the chain of events and highlight point of intervention (stoplight point from HANDOUT 17: Automatic Thoughts)

   d.   Repeat this exercise (three times total if time permits)

- Upon second and third graph, instruct participants to identify at what point they needed to assume responsibility for the situation (including their thoughts, feelings, and behaviors) and how they recognized the point to intervene (trigger).

4. **Utilize the Circle of Change (see HANDOUT 2 from Module I)**

   a. Emphasize past behavior led to negative outcomes, repeating past behavior will result in similarly negative outcomes, need to change behavior to change outcomes.

5. **Re-assign HOMEWORK 14: Challenging Automatic Thoughts Log**

   a. Provide multiple copies so participants do not limit their logging of automatic thoughts prior to the next session.

Session 10: Working Toward More Green Light— Changing Automatic Thoughts

Objective

This session will:

1. Continue educating participants about the effect of automatic thoughts on behavior (including behavior related to criminalness and mental illness)
2. Continue teaching participants how to monitor their automatic thoughts
3. Continue teaching participants how to challenge their automatic thoughts.

The primary objectives of this session are to ensure that participants continue to challenge their automatic thoughts and related criminal thinking. No new information is presented in this session, so participants can work on "overlearning" this information.

Materials

1. Blackboard or whiteboard (with chalk or markers) or flip chart (with markers)
2. Blank typing paper (minimum of two pages per participant)
3. QUIZ 2: Questions About Criminal Thinking
4. HOMEWORK 14: Challenging Automatic Thoughts Log

Session Content

1. **Ask for questions regarding Session 9 or HOMEWORK 14: Challenging Automatic Thoughts Log**
2. **Distribute QUIZ 2: Questions About Criminal Thinking**

    a.   Ask participants to complete the quiz
    b.   Score the quiz and discuss participant mastery of information.

3. **Review HOMEWORK 14: Challenging Automatic Thoughts Log**

    a.   Reinforce efforts to complete the homework

    •   Inform participants that effectively challenging their thinking is a skill (just like learning to monitor their thinking in previous sessions of this module)

    o   As with any skill, it takes time to develop the skill (e.g., riding a bike took time to learn).

    b.   Provide feedback to participants that did not complete the homework or were not effective in their record keeping

    •   Discuss barriers to completing homework and develop plan for working around those barriers.

    c.   Facilitate a group discussion on the difficulty and effectiveness of challenging their automatic thoughts

    •   Emphasize the effect on efforts toward recovery (long-term goals).

    d.   Reinforce potential for change to improve probability of recovery.

4. **Instruct participants to select one entry from their HOMEWORK 14: Challenging Automatic Thoughts Log and to graph the chain of events (flow chart as presented in Session 6)**

    a.   Any participant that did not complete the homework should be provided an example from another participants completed homework
    b.   Discuss the chain of events and highlight point of intervention (stoplight point from HANDOUT 17: Automatic Thoughts)
    c.   Repeat this exercise (three times total if time permits)

    •   Upon second and third graph, instruct participants to identify at what point they needed to assume responsibility for the situation (including their thoughts, feelings, and behaviors) and how they recognized the point to intervene (trigger)
    •   Utilize the Circle of Change (HANDOUT 2 from Module I)

o Emphasize past behavior led to negative outcomes, repeating past behavior will result in similarly negative outcomes, need to change behavior to change outcomes.

5. **Re-assign HOMEWORK 14: Challenging Automatic Thoughts Log**

   a. Provide multiple copies so participants do not limit their logging of automatic thoughts prior to the next session.

Session 11: More Working Toward More Green Light— Changing Automatic Thoughts

Objective

This session will:

1. Continue educating participants about the effect of automatic thoughts on behavior (including behavior related to criminalness and mental illness)
2. Continue teaching participants how to monitor their automatic thoughts
3. Continue teaching participants how to challenge their automatic thoughts.

The primary objective of this session is to ensure that participants continue to challenge their automatic thoughts and related criminal thinking. No new information is presented in this session, so participants can work on "overlearning" this information.

Materials

1. Blackboard or whiteboard (with chalk or markers) or flip chart (with markers)
2. Blank typing paper (minimum of two pages per participant)
3. HOMEWORK 14: Challenging Automatic Thoughts Log
4. HOMEWORK 15: Credit List of My Hard Work

Session Content

1. **Ask for questions regarding Session 10 or HOMEWORK 14: Challenging Automatic Thoughts Log**
2. **Review HOMEWORK 14: Challenging Automatic Thoughts Log**

   a. Have participants lead this review of HOMEWORK 14: Challenging Automatic Thoughts Log

- Provide feedback to participants about reinforcing (praising) and challenging one another's efforts at challenging criminal thinking

    o   Discuss barriers to participants' difficulty challenging and/or changing automatic thoughts.

- Help participants engage in a discussion on the difficulty and effectiveness of challenging their automatic thoughts

    o   Emphasize the effect on efforts toward recovery (long-term goals).

- Reinforce potential for change to improve probability of recovery.

3. **Instruct participants to select one entry from their Challenging Automatic Thoughts Log and to graph the chain of events (flow chart as presented in Session 3)**

    a. Any participant that did not complete the homework should be provided an example from another participant's completed homework
    b. Discuss the chain of events and highlight point of intervention (stoplight point from HANDOUT 17: Automatic Thoughts)
    c. Repeat this exercise (three times total if time permits)

        - Upon second and third graph, instruct participants to identify at what point they needed to assume responsibility for the situation (including their thoughts, feelings, and behaviors) and how they recognized the point to intervene (trigger)
        - Utilize the Circle of Change (HANDOUT 2 from Module I)

            o   Emphasize past behavior led to negative outcomes, repeating past behavior will result in similarly negative outcomes, need to change behavior to change outcomes.

4. **Re-assign HOMEWORK 14: Challenging Automatic Thoughts Log**

    a. Provide multiple copies so participants do not limit their logging of automatic thoughts prior to the next session.

5. **Assign HOMEWORK 15: Credit List of My Hard Work**

Session 12: Even More Working Toward More Green Light—Changing Automatic Thoughts

Objective

This session will:

1. Continue educating participants about the effect of automatic thoughts on behavior (including behavior related to criminalness and mental illness)
2. Continue teaching participants how to monitor their automatic thoughts
3. Continue teaching participants how to challenge their automatic thoughts.

The primary objectives of this session are to ensure that participants continue to challenge their automatic thoughts and related criminal thinking. No new information is presented in this session, so participants can work on "overlearning" this information.

Materials

1. Blackboard or whiteboard (with chalk or markers) or flip chart (with markers)
2. Blank typing paper (minimum of two pages per participant)
3. HOMEWORK 14: Challenging Automatic Thoughts Log
4. HOMEWORK 16: Not Challenging My Automatic Thoughts

Session Content

1. **Ask for questions regarding Session 11**
2. **Review HOMEWORK 15: Credit List of My Hard Work**

    a. Give positive reinforcement (e.g., praise) to each participant for any item on their credit list and reinforce their list as continued efforts toward recovery.

3. **Review HOMEWORK 14: Challenging Automatic Thoughts Log**

    a. Have participants lead this review of HOMEWORK 14: Challenging Automatic Thoughts Log

    - Provide feedback to participants about reinforcing (praising) and challenging one another's efforts at challenging criminal thinking

        o Discuss barriers to participants' difficulty challenging and/or changing automatic thoughts.

    - Help participants engage in a discussion on the difficulty and effectiveness of challenging their automatic thoughts

        o Emphasize effect on efforts toward recovery (long-term goals).

    - Reinforce potential for change to improve probability of recovery.

4. Instruct participants to select one entry from their Challenging Automatic Thoughts Log and to graph the chain of events (flow chart as presented in Session 3)

    a. Any participant that did not complete the homework should be provided an example from another participant's completed homework
    b. Discuss the chain of events and highlight point of intervention (stoplight point from HANDOUT 17: Automatic Thoughts)
    c. Repeat this exercise (three times total if time permits)

        •   Upon second and third graph, instruct participants to identify at what point they needed to assume responsibility for the situation (including their thoughts, feelings, and behaviors) and how they recognized the point to intervene (trigger)
        •   Utilize the Circle of Change (HANDOUT 2 from Module I)

            o   Emphasize past behavior led to negative outcomes, repeating past behavior will result in similarly negative outcomes, need to change behavior to change outcomes.

5. **Re-assign HOMEWORK 14: Challenging Automatic Thoughts Log**

    a. Provide multiple copies so participants do not limit their logging of automatic thoughts prior to the next session

6. **Assign HOMEWORK 16: Not Challenging My Automatic Thoughts**

Session 13: Putting It All Together—Changing My Criminal Thinking

Objective

This session will:

1. Help participants recognize pitfalls of failing to challenge automatic thoughts
2. Help participants revise their relapse plan.

The primary objective of this session is to reinforce participants' understanding of criminal thinking and automatic thoughts and strategies for challenging automatic thoughts, and including this information in an updated relapse plan.

Materials

1. Blackboard or whiteboard (with chalk or markers) or flip chart (with markers)

2. WORKSHEET 5: My Relapse Prevention Plan
3. "Thoughts and Attitudes" Graduation Certificates
4. Post-module Quiz

Session Content

1. **Ask for questions regarding Session 12**
2. **Review HOMEWORK 16: Not Challenging My Automatic Thoughts**

   a. Reinforce participants' recognition of missed opportunities to recognize or challenge their automatic thoughts
   b. Highlight similarities between participants' barriers to recognizing or challenging their automatic thoughts.

3. **Review the purpose of a relapse prevention plan**

   a. Explain to participants that their relapse prevention plan will include two components: issues of (1) mental illness and (2) criminalness
   b. Explain to participants that they will begin completing the criminalness portion of their relapse prevention plan in this session and will complete the plan during the course of the next six modules
   c. Refer participants back to information in Module II to complete the initial steps in their relapse prevention plan (note: although participants are working in a group, the specific steps in their plan should be individualized with your help).

4. **Help participants complete the following steps in their relapse prevention plan (WORKSHEET 5: My Relapse Prevention Plan)**

   a. My criminal thinking
   b. My early warning signs of criminal thinking
   c. Steps for challenging my criminal thinking
   d. People I will talk to when I become aware of my criminal thinking (include phone numbers).

8. **Distribute "Thoughts and Attitudes" graduation certificates**
9. **Complete Post-module Quiz**

16 Module IV
Medication Adherence

The aim of this treatment module is to facilitate CJ-PMI knowledge of the biological mechanisms of their disorder, the psychotropic medications they receive, the purpose of these medications, advantages and disadvantages of taking psychotropic medications, and strategies for coping with negative side effects to maximize treatment benefits. Finally, CJ-PMI will be educated on how to communicate with their treatment providers in an effective and meaningful manner to optimize their recovery. Consistent with the theoretical orientation of the *CLCO* program, this module incorporates a social-cognitive learning theory with structured exercises (including in and outside of group exercises) to educate participants and increase their awareness of the necessity of psychotropic medications to their recovery.

Content

The "Medication Adherence" module includes five sessions designed to educate participants about the necessity of their maintaining a regular psychopharmacological treatment regimen. The focus of this module is on educating participants on the biological mechanisms of schizophrenia, bipolar disorder, and major depressive disorder; the necessity of treating these disorders pharmacologically; and the benefits and side effects of various types of medications. Participants will also be educated about how to communicate with their physicians regarding their medications, specifically side effects they encounter, as well as coping strategies for undesirable side effects.

Session 1 provides an overview of the module including treatment goals, a review of participants' personal goals, and education about the biological mechanisms of schizophrenia, bipolar disorder, and major depressive disorder. This session will include pre-testing.

Session 2 reviews the advantages (benefits) and disadvantages (negative side effects) of psychotropic medications.

Session 3 teaches participants how to monitor their medications to assess for negative side effects.

Session 4 teaches participants skills for effectively communicating with health care providers about their medications and any problems they are having with their medications.

Session 5 teaches participants skills for coping with the negative side effects of their medications.

Treatment Process

The mechanism of change in this module is education based and didactic in nature. Similar to academic teaching, participants will be taught information and assigned tasks to facilitate their learning and retention of information for increased knowledge and awareness of their treatment needs. As the process for this module is psychoeducational in nature, each session is delivered with a cycle of content, in-class work, informational handouts, and homework.

Treatment Goals

The goal of the "Medication Adherence" module is knowledge accumulation and increased awareness of the benefits of an effective psychotropic treatment regimen.

The overarching treatment goals of the "Medication Adherence" module are that participants:

1. Learn the benefits of psychotropic medications for treating mental illness
2. Monitor psychotropic medication side effects
3. Develop skills to effectively communicate about their medications with their physician or prescriber
4. Develop strategies for coping with negative side effects.

Session 1: An Introduction to Medication Adherence

Objective

This session will:

1. Complete pre-testing
2. Review group rules
3. Review participants' personal goals
4. Introduce the "Medication Adherence" module and educate participants about the biological mechanisms of their mental illness.

The primary objective of this session is to educate participants about the biological mechanisms of schizophrenia, bipolar disorder, and major depressive disorder. This session will also include pre-testing and a review of group rules and participants' personal goals.

Materials

1. Blackboard or whiteboard (with chalk or markers) or flip chart (with markers)
2. Pre-module Quiz
3. HANDOUT 19: Biological Mechanisms of Mental Illness
4. HOMEWORK 17: What Are My Medications?

Session Content

1. **Complete Pre-module Quiz**
2. **Review group rules (write rules on board and review verbally)**

   a. HANDOUT 1: Rules of the Pool

3. **Review participant's personal goals**

   a. Each participant reviews their personal goals aloud to the group

4. **Review the Biological Mechanisms of Mental Illness**

   a. HANDOUT 19: Biological Mechanisms of Mental Illness

   - Review biological mechanisms of mental illness generally
   - Review biological mechanisms of schizophrenia
   - Review biological mechanisms of bipolar disorder
   - Review biological mechanisms of major depressive disorder.

5. **Discuss importance of psychotropic medications for treating these biological mechanisms**

   a. Explain different types of psychotropic medications

   - Antipsychotic
   - Antidepressant
   - Mood stabilizers
   - Antianxiety medications.

   b. Some disorders require multiple types of medications

   - Mood stabilizer and antidepressant
   - Antipsychotic and antidepressant
   - Antipsychotic, antidepressant, and antianxiety
   - Goal of psychotropic medication = increased likelihood for recovery.

6. **Assign HOMEWORK 17: What Are My Medications?**

Session 2: Psychotropic Medications: Benefits and Side Effects

Objective

This session will:

1. Educate participants about the benefits of psychotropic medications
2. Educate participants about the negative side effects associated with psychotropic medications.

The primary objectives of this session are to educate participants about issues related to the advantages and disadvantages of using psychotropic medications.

Materials

1. Blackboard or whiteboard (with chalk or markers) or flip chart (with markers)
2. HANDOUT 20: Medications: Advantages and Disadvantages
3. HANDOUT 21: Antipsychotic Medications
4. HANDOUT 22: Antidepressant Medications
5. HANDOUT 23: Mood Stabilizer Medications
6. HOMEWORK 18: Why I Take My Medications

Session Content

1. **Review Session 1 and review HOMEWORK 17: What Are My Medications?**

   a. Ask for questions regarding Session 1 and provide feedback to participants regarding HOMEWORK 17

2. **Explain that medications that treat mental illness have both advantages and disadvantages**

   a. Distribute and review HANDOUT 20: Medications: Advantages and Disadvantages

3. **Explain that medications designed to treat different mental illnesses have different benefits and side effects**

   a. Distribute and review HANDOUT 21: Antipsychotic Medications
   b. Distribute and review HANDOUT 22: Antidepressant Medications
   c. Distribute and review HANDOUT 23: Mood Stabilizer Medications

4. **Ask participants to share the advantages they've experienced from psychotropic medications**

5. Ask participants to share the negative side effects they've experienced with psychotropic medications
6. Assign HOMEWORK 18: Why I Take My Medications

Session 3: Monitoring and Learning to Cope With Negative Effects of Medications and Barriers to Medication Compliance

Objective

This session will:

1. Teach participants effective strategies for monitoring their medications for the presence of negative side effects
2. Introduce the stoplight as a mechanism for monitoring early warning signs (yellow light) and triggers (red light) for monitoring negative side effects and avoiding medication noncompliance.

The primary objectives of the session are to teach participants how to monitor their medications and use the stoplight as a framework for conceptualizing their medication adherence.

Materials

1. Blackboard or whiteboard (with chalk or markers) or flip chart (with markers)
2. HANDOUT 24: Effective Strategies for Monitoring My Side Effects
3. HANDOUT 25: Coping With Side Effects
4. HANDOUT 26: Early Warning Signs and Triggers for Medication Non-compliance
5. HOMEWORK 19: My Early Warning Signs and Triggers for Medication Non-compliance

Session Content

1. **Collect HOMEWORK 19 and briefly review content from Session 2**

   a. Ask for questions regarding Session 2 or HANDOUT 20: Medications: Advantages and Disadvantages

2. **Discuss strategies for monitoring medication side effects**

   a. Discuss (remind) participants that they are responsible for their recovery, which includes monitoring their medication side effects

   • Medication non-compliance is a lack of responsibility and a symptom of criminalness.

b. Distribute HANDOUT 24: Effective Strategies for Monitoring My Side Effects
c. Review handout and seek feedback from participants about their experiences

  • e.g., to whom they talk when they have negative side effects, how often they monitor their side effects.

3. **Coping With Side Effects**

   a. Distribute HANDOUT 25: Coping With Side Effects
   b. Review listed side effects and coping strategies
   c. Help participants identify additional coping strategies to those already listed
   d. Discuss (and have participants list) other side effects and develop a list of coping strategies.

4. **Review Early Warning Signs and Triggers for Medication Non-Compliance**

   a. Review Early Warning Signs and Triggers from the "Mental Illness and Criminalness Awareness" module
   b. Distribute HANDOUT 26: Early Warning Signs and Triggers for Medication Non-compliance
   c. Review handout and seek feedback from participants about their experiences

  • e.g., early warning signs and triggers they've become aware of over the years.

5. **Assign HOMEWORK 19: My Early Warning Signs and Triggers for Medication Non-compliance**

Session 4: Communicating With My Health Care Professionals

Objective

This session will:

1. Educate participants about the necessity of actively communicating with health care providers to achieve recovery
2. Teach participants skills for effectively communicating with their health care provider regarding the advantages and disadvantages of their medications.

The primary objective of the session is to educate participants on how to communicate with their treatment providers in an effective and meaningful manner to optimize their recovery.

Materials

1. Blackboard or whiteboard (with chalk or markers) or flip chart (with markers)
2. HANDOUT 27: Medication Awareness
3. HOMEWORK 20: Getting My Needs Met With Medication

Session Content

1. Review content from Session 3.
2. Ask for questions regarding Session 3 and review HOMEWORK 19: My Early Warning Signs and Triggers for Medication Non-compliance

   a. Spend more time than usual reviewing HOMEWORK 19. Given the significance of identifying early warning signs and triggers for medication non-compliance, spend more time than usual reviewing this homework.

3. Discuss with participants the advantages of actively participating in their treatment regimen by discussing their medications and the effects of their medications with their doctor

   a. Have participants discuss times when they had problems with medications and did not talk with their doctor

      • What happened during such times?
      • How did this contribute to relapse or a loss of recovery?

   b. Distribute and review HANDOUT 27: Medication Awareness

4. Assign HOMEWORK 20: Getting My Needs Met With Medication

Session 5: Medication Adherence and My Relapse Prevention Plan

Objective

This session will:

1. Help participants begin to develop their relapse prevention plan.

The primary objective of the session is to help participants begin to develop a comprehensive relapse prevention plan (as presented in Module II) for achieving recovery. This session will begin the development of the plan and subsequent modules will add to the plan in a sequential manner. This session focuses on early warning signs and triggers to relapse as well as issues related to medication adherence.

Materials

1. Blackboard or whiteboard (with chalk or markers) or flip chart (with markers)
2. WORKSHEET 5: My Relapse Prevention Plan
3. "Medication Adherence" Graduation Certificate
4. Post-module Quiz

Session Content

1. Review HOMEWORK 20: Getting My Needs Met With Medication
2. Ask for questions regarding Session 5 and ensure participants have brought all previous handouts/homework
3. Help participants complete the following steps in their relapse prevention plan (WORKSHEET 5: My Relapse Prevention Plan):

   a. My psychiatric triggers
   b. My early warning signs of psychiatric relapse
   c. Medications for my mental illness
   d. Side effects of these medications that I struggle with include
   e. People I will talk to when the side effects are too severe or when I think about going off my medications (include phone numbers).

5. Complete Post-module Quiz

17 Module V

Coping With Mental Illness and Criminalness

The aim of this module is to educate and teach participants how to manage their problems, such as stress, boredom, and symptoms that affect their mental health functioning and criminalness. The focus of this module is reinforcing recognition of early warning signs of relapse (mental health and criminal), recognizing sources of stress and developing effective stress management strategies, and further developing a relapse prevention plan for mental illness and criminalness. The focus of the intervention will be on identifying the need for early interventions, coping with stress and persistent symptoms of mental illness (e.g., cognitive process, mood disturbance) and criminalness (e.g., proneness to boredom, antisocial attitudes), and developing healthy and prosocial habits. Consistent with the program focus, this module relies on psychoeducation to teach participants about the signs of stress and effective stress, symptom and criminalness management strategies.

Content

The "Coping With Mental Illness and Criminalness" module includes eight sessions designed to help participants recognize their sources of stress, implement effective stress management strategies, and develop effective coping strategies for dealing with symptoms of mental illness and criminalness.

Session 1 presents stress as a red light and helps participants become more aware of the physical and emotional signs of stress. This session will include pre-testing.

Session 2 continues to help participants increase their awareness of stress by helping them identify sources of stress. This module also begins teaching participants effective strategies for coping with stress.

Sessions 3 and 4 teach participants effective strategies for managing their stress. Specifically, participants are taught deep breathing techniques, progressive muscle relaxation strategies, positive imagery techniques, and strategies for using positive self-talk. Participants will learn these strategies in session, and assigned homework will require them to practice these strategies in their everyday functioning.

Session 5, 6, and 7 help participants identify their common everyday problems and symptoms associated with their mental illness and criminalness. In these sessions the therapist will also teach participants effective strategies for coping with these problems and symptoms. Emphasis is placed on overlearning the recommended strategies so they become natural responses for participants when dealing with problems and symptoms in the real world.

Session 8 continues the development of the participant's formal relapse prevention plan.

Treatment Process

The "Coping With Mental Illness and Criminalness" module is grounded in traditional cognitive-behavioral theory with emphasis on participant's skill development for coping with their mental health symptoms and criminalness. Emphasis is placed on learning about stress, symptoms of stress, and cognitive-behavioral skills for coping with stress. This module also integrates a psychoeducational format with structured learning activities to include in-class work, informational handouts, and homework for knowledge and skill development specifically developed to teach participants how to recognize and cope with symptoms of stress, mental illness, and criminalness.

Treatment Goals

The overarching treatment goals of the "Coping With Mental Illness and Criminalness" module are that participants will:

1. Understand and recognize sources and symptoms of stress in their lives
2. Develop skills for coping with stress
3. Develop skills for coping with their symptoms of mental illness and criminalness as identified in Module II ("Mental Illness and Criminalness Awareness").

Session 1: Coping With Mental Illness and Criminalness: Getting Started

Objective

This session will:

1. Complete pre-testing
2. Review group rules

3. Review participants' personal goals
4. Introduce the "Coping With Mental Illness and Criminalness" module
5. Teach participants about the negative effects of stress
6. Help participants begin to recognize their personal signs of stress.

The primary objectives of this session are to reinforce to participants the negative effects of stress on mental illness and criminalness and to help participants begin to recognize their signs of being under stress. This session will include pre-testing and a review of group rules and participants' personal goals.

Materials

1. Blackboard or whiteboard (with chalk or markers) or flip chart (with markers)
2. Pre-module Quiz
3. WORKSHEET 7: Recognizing My Stress
4. HOMEWORK 21: Signs of Stress Checklist

Session Content

1. **Complete Pre-module Quiz**
2. **Review group rules (write rules on board and review verbally— optional)**

   a. HANDOUT 1: Rules of the Pool

3. **Review participant's personal goals**

   a. Each participant reviews their personal goals aloud to the group

4. **Review of stress and its role in mental illness and criminalness**

   a. Define stress

   • Include discussion of stress as a red light
   • Sign of stress is a yellow light
   • Effectively coping with stress is a green light.

   b. Teach the role of stress in your recovery

   • Why is stress relevant to mental illness?
   • Why is stress relevant to criminalness?

   c. Distribute WORKSHEET 7: Recognizing My Stress

5. **Assign HOMEWORK 21: Signs of Stress Checklist**

Session 2: Preventing Stress

Objective

This session will:

1. Continue to help participants identify their sources of stress
2. Begin to teach participants stress management strategies.

The primary objectives of this session are to continue educating participants with mental illness about their source of stress (reinforcing how stress negatively impacts their recovery process) as well as begin to provide participants strategies for managing their stress.

Materials

1. Blackboard or whiteboard (with chalk or markers) or flip chart (with markers)
2. WORKSHEET 8: Normal Life Events Are Stressful
3. WORKSHEET 9: Role of Daily Hassles
4. HANDOUT 28: Strategies for Preventing Stress
5. HOMEWORK 22: Implementing Strategies for Preventing Stress

Session Content

1. **Review Session 1 and review HOMEWORK 21: Signs of Stress Checklist**

    a. Reinforce participants' recognition of their stressors
    b. Discuss their signs of stress as yellow lights (that is, each sign checked is a yellow light or an indicator that the participant may become stressed out).

2. **Discuss how life events are also indicators (yellow light) of stress**

    a. Distribute and discuss WORKSHEET 8: Normal Life Events Are Stressful
    b. Discuss results of WORKSHEET 9: Role of Daily Hassles

3. **Discuss stressful life sitations**

    a. Most stressful life situation participants experienced in the past year (review WORKSHEET 8 as necessary)
    b. Most stressful daily hassles participants experienced in the month before their incarceration (review WORKSHEET 9 as necessary)
    c. Signs participants have noticed that indicate they are experiencing stress (review HOMEWORK 21: Signs of Stress Checklist as necessary).

4. Ask participants to share how they coped with the stressful life situations, daily hassles and signs of stress discussed in #3
5. Inform participants that it is essential to their recovery and attainment of their personal goals that they develop responsibility for managing their stress

   a. Distribute and review HANDOUT 28: Strategies for Preventing Stress

6. **Assign HOMEWORK 22: Implementing Strategies for Preventing Stress**

Session 3: Managing Stress

Objective

This session will:

1. Teach participants effective strategies for managing stress.

The primary objective of this session is to teach participants relaxation strategies such as deep breathing, muscle relaxation, imagery, and positive self-talk.

Materials

1. Blackboard or whiteboard (with chalk or markers) or flip chart (with markers)
2. HANDOUT 29: Deep Breathing
3. HANDOUT 30: Muscle Relaxation
4. HANDOUT 31: Positive Imagery
5. HANDOUT 32: Positive Self-Talk
6. HOMEWORK 23: Implementing Stress Management Strategies— Part I

Session Content

1. **Ask for questions regarding Session 2 or HOMEWORK 22: Implementing Strategies for Preventing Stress**

   a. Review strategies used to cope with stress and the effectiveness of these strategies (HOMEWORK 22)

2. **Inform participants that they have begun to recognize the sources of stress, and it is now time to begin developing effective strategies for coping with stress**

3. Discuss the four short-term strategies for managing stress in the moment

   a. Explain the concept and benefits of deep breathing

      • Distribute HANDOUT 29 and practice deep breathing.

   b. Explain the concept and benefits of muscle relaxation

      • Distribute HANDOUT 30 and practice muscle relaxation.

   c. Explain the concept and benefits of imagery

      • Distribute HANDOUT 31 and practice positive imagery exercise.

   d. Explain the concept and benefits of positive self-talk

      • Distribute HANDOUT 32 and practice positive self-talk.

4. Assign HOMEWORK 23: Implementing Stress Management Strategies—Part I

Session 4: More Managing Stress

Objective

This session will:

1. Continue helping participants develop effective strategies for managing stress.

The primary objective of this session is to refine participants' use of relaxation strategies such as deep breathing, muscle relaxation, imagery, and positive self-talk.

Materials

1. Blackboard or whiteboard (with chalk or markers) or flip chart (with markers)
2. HANDOUT 33: Examples of Coping With Stress
3. HOMEWORK 24: Implementing Stress Management Strategies— Part II

Session Content

1. Review content from Session 3
2. Ask for questions regarding Session 3 and review HOMEWORK 23: Implementing Stress Management Strategies—Part I

   a. Spend time reviewing the effectiveness of these strategies for reducing stress (increasing relaxation)

b.   Explore resistance or barriers to implementing these stress management strategies

- Challenge participants' resistance to utilizing these strategies as criminalness and discuss necessity of managing stress

3.   **Practice the four short-term strategies for managing stress in the moment again**

a.   Review HANDOUT 29 and practice deep breathing
b.   Review HANDOUT 30 and practice muscle relaxation
c.   Review HANDOUT 31 and practice positive imagery exercise
d.   Review HANDOUT 32 and practice positive self-talk.

4.   **Provide examples of when they might use these coping strategies**

a.   Distribute and review HANDOUT 33: Examples of Coping With Stress.

5.   **Assign HOMEWORK 24: Implementing Stress Management Strategies—Part II**

Session 5: Coping With Common Problems, and Symptoms of Mental Illness and Criminalness

Objective

This session will:

1.   Teach participants effective strategies for coping with the problems and symptoms of mental illness and criminalness.

The primary objective of this session is to teach participants effective strategies for coping with a myriad of problems including disturbances of thought, negative affect, negative symptoms that are associated with loss of functioning, psychosis, substance abuse, criminalness, and any other problem or symptom that interferes with their daily functioning.

Materials

1.   Blackboard or whiteboard (with chalk or markers) or flip chart (with markers)
2.   WORKSHEET 10: Checklist of Common Problems and Symptoms
3.   HANDOUT 34: Strategies for Coping With Disturbances of Thought
4.   HANDOUT 35: Strategies for Coping With Negative Affect
5.   HANDOUT 36: Strategies for Coping With Negative Symptoms
6.   HANDOUT 37: Strategies for Coping With Psychotic Symptoms

7. HANDOUT 38: Strategies for Coping With Substance Abuse
8. HANDOUT 39: Strategies for Coping With Criminalness
9. HOMEWORK 25: Coping With My Problems and Symptoms

Session Content

1. **Ask for questions regarding Session 3 or HOMEWORK 24: Implementing Stress Management Strategies—Part II**

   a. Review strategies used to cope with stress and the effectiveness of these strategies (HOMEWORK 24: Implementing Stress Management Strategies—Part II)

2. **Explain that everyone (all people) has different problems and symptoms that they must deal with and summarize the types of problems (category of problem in HANDOUT 33: Examples of Coping With Stress) in everyday terms for the participants.**

   a. Distribute WORKSHEET 10: Checklist of Common Problems and Symptoms
   b. Review participant responses helping each participant identify their primary type (category) of problems/symptoms.

3. **Inform participants that there are strategies for dealing with their everyday problems and symptoms. Their task is to identify what works for them and to begin using these strategies in their everyday life.**

   a. Discuss strategies for coping with disturbances of thought

      • Distribute HANDOUT 34: Strategies for Coping With Disturbances of Thought and teach/practice the strategies

   b. Discuss strategies for coping with negative affect

      • Distribute HANDOUT 35: Strategies for Coping With Negative Affect and teach/practice the strategies

   c. Discuss strategies for coping with negative symptoms

      • Distribute HANDOUT 36: Strategies for Coping With Negative Symptoms and teach/practice the strategies

   d. Discuss strategies for coping with psychotic symptoms

      • Distribute HANDOUT 37: Strategies for Coping With Psychotic Symptoms and teach/practice the strategies

   e. Discuss strategies for coping with substance abuse

      • Distribute HANDOUT 38: Strategies for Coping With Substance Abuse and teach/practice the strategies

f.   Discuss strategies for coping with criminalness

•   Distribute HANDOUT 39: Strategies for Coping With Criminalness and teach/practice the strategies

4.   **Assign HOMEWORK 25: Coping With My Problems and Symptoms**

Session 6: More Coping With Common Problems, and Symptoms of Mental Illness and Criminalness

Objective

This session will:

1.   Continue helping participants develop effective strategies for coping with the problems and symptoms of mental illness and criminalness.

The primary objective of this session is to refine participants' use of coping strategies for common problems and symptoms of mental illness.

Materials

1.   Blackboard or whiteboard (with chalk or markers) or flip chart (with markers)
2.   HANDOUT 40: Examples of Coping With Stress
3.   HOMEWORK 25: Coping With My Problems and Symptoms

Session Content

1.   **Ask for questions regarding Session 5 and review HOMEWORK 19: Coping With My Problems and Symptoms—Part I**

a.   Spend time reviewing the effectiveness of these strategies for reducing problems/symptoms
b.   Explore resistance or barriers to implementing these coping strategies

•   Challenge participant's resistance to utilizing these strategies as criminalness and discuss necessity of managing their problems and symptoms.

3.   **Review and practice the coping strategies in HANDOUTS 34–39 (stress the importance of overlearning information)**

a.   Review HANDOUT 34: Strategies for Coping With Disturbances of Thought and teach/practice the strategies
b.   Review HANDOUT 35: Strategies for Coping With Negative Affect and teach/practice the strategies

    c. Review HANDOUT 36: Strategies for Coping With Negative Symptoms and teach/practice the strategies

    d. Review HANDOUT 37: Strategies for Coping With Psychotic Symptoms and teach/practice the strategies

    e. Review HANDOUT 38: Strategies for Coping With Substance Abuse and teach/practice the strategies

    f. Review HANDOUT 39: Strategies for Coping With Criminalness and teach/practice the strategies.

4. **Provide examples of when they might use these coping strategies**

    a. Distribute and review HANDOUT 40: Examples of Coping With Stress

5. **Re-assign HOMEWORK 25: Coping With My Problems and Symptoms**

Session 7: Still More Coping With Common Problems, and Symptoms of Mental Illness and Criminalness

Objective

This session will:

1. Continue helping participants develop effective strategies for coping with the problems and symptoms of mental illness and criminalness.

The primary objective of this session is to refine participant's use of coping strategies for common problems and symptoms of mental illness.

Materials

1. Blackboard or whiteboard (with chalk or markers) or flip chart (with markers)
2. HOMEWORK 24: Implementing Stress Management Strategies— Part II
3. HOMEWORK 25: Coping With My Problems and Symptoms

Session Content

1. **Ask for questions regarding Session 6 and review HOMEWORK 25: Coping With My Problems and Symptoms**

    a. Spend time reviewing the effectiveness of these strategies for reducing problems/symptoms

    b. Explore resistance or barriers to implementing these coping strategies

        • Challenge participant's resistance to utilizing these strategies as criminalness and discuss necessity of managing their problems and symptoms.

2. Review and practice the coping strategies in HANDOUTS 34–39 (again stress the importance of overlearning information)

    a. Review HANDOUT 34: Strategies for Coping With Disturbances of Thought and teach/practice the strategies

    b. Review HANDOUT 35: Strategies for Coping With Negative Affect and teach/practice the strategies

    c. Review HANDOUT 36: Strategies for Coping With Negative Symptoms and teach/practice the strategies

    d. Review HANDOUT 37: Strategies for Coping With Psychotic Symptoms and teach/practice the strategies

    e. Review HANDOUT 38: Strategies for Coping With Substance Abuse and teach/practice the strategies

    f. Review HANDOUT 39: Strategies for Coping With Criminalness and teach/practice the strategies.

6. Assign homework to reinforce (overlearn) coping strategies

    a. Re-assign HOMEWORK 24: Implementing Stress Management Strategies—Part II

    b. Re-assign HOMEWORK 25: Coping With My Problems and Symptoms

    c. Instruct participants to bring all handouts and completed homework from this module to the next session (final session of this module) to continue development of their relapse prevention plan.

Session 8: Coping With Mental Illness and Criminalness: My Relapse Prevention Plan

Objective

This session will:

1. Help participants continue developing their relapse prevention plan.

The primary objective of the session is to help participants further their development of a comprehensive relapse prevention plan (as presented in Module II and continued from Module III) for achieving recovery. This session incorporates how to cope with mental illness and criminalness into the relapse prevention plan.

Materials

1. Blackboard or whiteboard (with chalk or markers) or flip chart (with markers)
2. WORKSHEET 11: My Relapse Prevention Plan
3. "Coping With Mental Illness and Criminalness" Graduation Certificate
4. Post-module Quiz

Session Content

1. Ask for questions regarding Session 7 and ensure participants have brought all previous handouts/homework
2. Review the purpose of a relapse prevention plan
3. Remind participants that their relapse prevention plan includes two components: issues of (1) mental illness and (2) criminalness
4. Refer participants back to information in Module IV (handouts and completed homework) to complete the presented steps in their relapse prevention plan
5. Help participants complete the following steps in their relapse prevention plan (WORKSHEET 11: My Relapse Prevention Plan). Note: although participants are working in a group, the specific steps in their plan should be individualized with your help

    a. My signs of stress
    b. My daily hassles
    c. Strategies I will use to cope with stress and daily hassles
    d. My common problems and symptoms
    e. Strategies I will use to cope with my problems.

6. **Complete Post-module Quiz and Modular Assessment**

    a. "Coping With Mental Illness and Criminalness" Questionnaire

18 Module VI
Emotions Management

Building a Motivation to Manage Emotions

The aim of this treatment module is to educate and teach CJ-PMI to understand and recognize their negative affect and how negative affect impacts their psychiatric symptomatology and criminal propensity. Consistent with the theoretical orientation of the *Changing Lives and Changing Outcomes* (CLCO) program, this module incorporates a social-cognitive learning theory with structured exercises (including in and outside of group exercises) to facilitate CJ-PMI awareness. By understanding their negative affect, the role that this area can have in their psychiatric functioning and criminal activities, CJ-PMI will be better equipped to facilitate improved outcomes including reduced criminal and psychiatric recidivism (e.g., absence of imprisonment, fewer jail days, fewer hospital days, improved psychosocial functioning—more good days). The "Emotions Management" module focuses on anger, anxiety, and depression. Each of these areas can have a role in criminal and psychiatric recidivism.

Content

The "Emotions Management" module includes ten sessions to help participants understand and change their functioning in the areas of anger, anxiety, and depression.

Session 1 provides a readiness to change review for the areas of anger, anxiety, and depression. There is an emphasis on better emotions management.

Session 2 will help participants identify cues that result in anger.

Session 3 will assist participants with the skills needed to change the thought patterns associated with anger arousal.

Session 4 will assist participants to examine behavioral causes of anger and suggest alternative habits to deal with anger arousal.

Session 5 will examine the social settings that are associated with anger.

Session 6 will provide skills to assess and reduce anxiety. These will include progressive muscle relaxation and breathing techniques.

Session 7 will provide the thinking skills that assist with the reduction of anxiety.

Session 8 focuses on depression and provides the client strategies for participating in environments that are a source of pleasure and have a green light.

Session 9 will develop potential daily pleasant activities that will assist in preventing a drift toward negative emotions.

Session 10 will discuss the thoughts/feelings that contribute to the participant's chain toward depression. Strategies to change thoughts/feelings are presented.

Treatment Process

As noted in *CLCO*, all modules will be offered in a psychoeducational group setting. Although the theoretical orientation of the program integrates cognitive-behavioral and social-learning paradigms, the focus in this module is developing understanding, management skills, and the process of change in the area of negative affect. The goal of the "Emotions Management" module is to understand, manage, and change negative affect. This module's mechanism of change is based on the model, with a focus on the affective component. In addition, the traffic light heuristic is used throughout the module. As the process for this module is psychoeducational in nature, each session is delivered with a cycle of content, in-class work, information handouts, and homework. Pre- and post-testing is conducted to measure both constructs and content of the group.

Treatment Goals

The overarching treatment goals of the "Emotions Management" module are to assist the CJ-PMI to:

1. Manage anger, anxiety, and depression
2. Change the impact of anger, anxiety, and depression.

Session 1: Getting Ready to Change

Objective

This session will:

1. Help participants see how ready they are to change in the areas of anger, anxiety, and negative feelings.

The primary objective of this session is to review participants' readiness for change with regard to emotions of anger, anxiety, and depressed mood. This session will include the modular pre-test.

Materials

1. Blackboard or whiteboard (with chalk or markers) or flip chart (with markers)
2. Pre-module Quiz
3. HANDOUT 41: Precontemplation Stage of Change
4. WORKSHEET 12: Scenarios—Outside or Inside Reasons
5. WORKSHEET 13: Your Past Successes
6. WORKSHEET 14: Readiness Ruler—Emotions Management
7. HOMEWORK 26: Better Emotions Management

Session Content

1. Complete Pre-module Quiz
2. Discuss that it is common for emotions to impact our ability to reach our goals. Discuss with participants that changing emotions is difficult.

   a. The reasons for change need to be stated. Some may involve deeply felt emotional pain. Be considerate of these emotional antecedents.

   Therapist Note: Have participants identify reasons for change while you write them on the board or flip chart.

   ---

   b. Some participants may not be ready to change. Going through the stages of change is essential for those who will have a difficult time to change.

3. Distribute HANDOUT 41: Precontemplation Stage of Change

   a. Discuss the main points of the handout.
   b. Emphasize the difference between "outside reasons" and "inside reasons."

4. Distribute WORKSHEET 12: Scenarios—Outside or Inside Reasons
5. Distribute WORKSHEET 13: Your Past Successes
6. Distribute WORKSHEET 14: Readiness Ruler—Emotions Management
7. Assign HOMEWORK 26: Better Emotions Management

Session 2: Anger Arousal

Objective

This session will:

1. Introduce the idea of arousal and identify the cues to arousal in each of the Circle of Change areas.

The primary objective of this session is to teach participants to identify their cues to anger and introduce skills for coping with anger.

Materials

1.   Blackboard or whiteboard (with chalk or markers) or flip chart (with markers)
2.   WORKSHEET 15: Arousal
3.   HANDOUT 42: Contributors to Anger Arousal
4.   HANDOUT 43: The Lights
5.   WORKSHEET 16: Red Light Areas That Contribute to Anger Arousal
6.   HOMEWORK 27: Anger Event

Session Content

1.   Review HOMEWORK 26: Better Emotions Management

     a.   Be sure to discuss the "inside reasons" of the answers.

2.   **Review the benefits of managing our emotions and gain participants' commitment to the module**
3.   **Distribute WORKSHEET 15: Arousal**

     a.   Point out that many bodily responses are the same for many emotions.

          •   Our bodies react in the same way no matter what we feel.
          •   How we feel depends on how we view the situation.

     b.   This worksheet can be done individually in the group setting or as a group.

4.   **Distribute HANDOUT 42: Contributors to Anger Arousal**
5.   **Distribute HANDOUT 43: The Lights**
6.   **Distribute WORKSHEET 16: Red Light Areas That Contribute to Anger Arousal**
7.   **Assign HOMEWORK 27: Anger Event**

Session 3: Thoughts and Anger Arousal

Objective

This session will:

1.   Explore skills to change the thought patterns that contribute to anger arousal.

The primary objective of this session is to help participants develop the skills needed to change their thought patterns associated with anger arousal.

Materials

1. Blackboard or whiteboard (with chalk or markers) or flip chart (with markers)
2. HANDOUT 44: RED 123
3. WORKSHEET 17: Stopping Red Thoughts
4. WORKSHEET 18: Dealing With Yellow Thoughts
5. HOMEWORK 28: A Red Thought—Anger Arousal

Session Content

1. **Review HOMEWORK 27: Anger Event**
2. **Explain to participants that when a red light thought occurs it must be disputed**
3. **Distribute HANDOUT 44: RED 123**

    a. Ensure participants have grasped this before moving on.

5. **Distribute WORKSHEET 17: Stopping Red Thoughts**

    a. You may want to use more than one red thought
    b. Have a participant identify a red thought, then work through the worksheet as a group.

6. **Distribute WORKSHEET 18: Dealing With Yellow Thoughts**
8. **Assign HOMEWORK 28: A Red Thought—Anger Arousal**

Session 4: Anger Habits

Objective

This session will:

1. Examine the behavioral causes of anger and suggest alternative habits to deal with anger arousal.

The primary objective of this session is to help participants examine behavioral causes of anger and suggest alternative habits to deal with anger arousal.

Materials

1. Blackboard or whiteboard (with chalk or markers) or flip chart (with markers)
2. HANDOUT 45: Three Behavioral Responses to Anger Arousal
3. WORKSHEET 19: Case Study—Jim
4. HANDOUT 46: Habits That Reduce Anger Arousal

5. HANDOUT 47: Basic Rights of Assertive Communication
6. WORKSHEET 20: Role Play—Assertion Skills
7. HOMEWORK 29: Habit Responses to Anger Arousal

Session Content

1. Review HOMEWORK 28: A Red Thought—Anger Arousal
2. Distribute HANDOUT 45: Three Behavioral Responses to Anger Arousal
3. Distribute WORKSHEET 19: Case Study—Jim
4. Distribute HANDOUT 46: Habits That Reduce Anger Arousal

   a. Discuss how these habits can apply to the participant's past situation

5. Distribute HANDOUT 47: Basic Rights of Assertive Communication

   a. We have basic communication rights, whether we exercise them or not.

6. Distribute WORKSHEET 20: Role Play—Assertion Skills

   a. By this session you will have some understanding of the participants. Pick situations for role play that are relevant for your participants.

5. Assign HOMEWORK 29: Habit Responses to Anger Arousal

Session 5: Environmental Setting/Cues Leading to Anger Arousal

Objective

This session will:

1. Examine social settings that are associated with anger.

The primary objective of this session is to facilitate participants examination of social settings that are associated with anger, and to teach exit strategies when these social settings are encountered.

Materials

1. Blackboard or whiteboard (with chalk or markers) or flip chart (with markers)
2. Pre-module Quiz
3. HANDOUT 48: Environmental Cues That Lead to Anger

4. WORKSHEET 21: Evaluating Anger Environments
5. WORKSHEET 22: Exiting Skills
6. HOMEWORK 30: Anger 123

Session Content

1. **Review HOMEWORK 29: Habit Responses to Anger Arousal**
2. **Distribute HANDOUT 48: Environmental Cues That Lead to Anger**

    a. Discuss which ones apply to the participant and why.

3. **Distribute WORKSHEET 21: Evaluating Anger Environments**
4. **Distribute WORKSHEET 22: Exiting Skills**

    a. Role-play with two participants at a time. Try to use the participants' red light environments. Try also to incorporate the assertive skills from the last session.

5. **Assign HOMEWORK 30: Anger 123**

Session 6: Reducing Anxiety Levels: Relaxation

Objective

This session will:

1. Help participants develop two relaxation skills.

The primary objective of this session is to teach participants skills to assess and reduce anxiety.

Materials

1. Blackboard or whiteboard (with chalk or markers) or flip chart (with markers)
2. WORKSHEET 23: Assessing Anxiety
3. HANDOUT 49: Progressive Muscle Relaxation—Skill
4. WORKSHEET 24: Rate Your Body Tension
5. HANDOUT 50: Progressive Muscle Relaxation—Skill Guide
6. HANDOUT 51: Breathing Strategies
7. HOMEWORK 31: Practice PMR and Breathing

Session Content

1. Review **HOMEWORK 30: Anger 123**
2. Discuss **WORKSHEET 23: Assessing Anxiety**

3. Distribute and discuss HANDOUT 49: Progressive Muscle Relaxation
4. Distribute and have each participant complete WORKSHEET 24: Rate Your Body Tension

   a. Make four copies per participant for this session.

5. Using the HANDOUT 50: Progressive Muscle Relaxation—Skill Guide, conduct a progressive muscle relaxation session
6. Complete WORKSHEET 24: Rate Your Body Tension after the progressive muscle relaxation session
7. Distribute and read HANDOUT 51: Breathing Strategies

   a. Practice breathing skills
   b. The use of the hands on the chest and stomach are only needed to help the participant train. Once they are confident that deep breathing is occurring, the use of the hands is not necessary.

8. Using the HANDOUT 50: Progressive Muscle Relaxation—Skill Guide, do a second progressive muscle relaxation session
9. Complete WORKSHEET 24: Rate Your Body Tension
10. Assign HOMEWORK 31: Practice Progressive Muscle Relaxation and Breathing

Session 7: Thinking Skills That Reduce Anxiety

Objective

This session will:

1. Introduce thinking skills that assist with the reduction of anxiety.

The primary objective of this session is to teach participants cognitive skills that assist with anxiety reduction.

Materials

1. Blackboard or whiteboard (with chalk or markers) or flip chart (with markers)
2. HANDOUT 52: Thoughts That Lead to Anxiety
3. WORKSHEET 25: Your Chain to Anxiety
4. HOMEWORK 32: Final Copy of My Chain

Session Content

1. Review HOMEWORK 31: Practice Progressive Muscle Relaxation and Breathing

    a.   Emphasize the benefits of practicing these skills.

2. **Distribute HANDOUT 52: Thoughts That Lead to Anxiety**

    a.   Discuss the categories of thoughts that lead to anxiety
    b.   Have the participants give their own examples in each category.

3. **Distribute WORKSHEET 25: Your Chain to Anxiety**

    a.   Present an example of the chain.

4. **Assign HOMEWORK 32: Final Copy of My Chain**

Session 8: Changing Environments—Depression

Objective

This session will:

1. Assist the participant in changing and participating in environments that are a source of pleasure and have a green light.

The primary objective of this session is to teach participants the role of environment in contributing to a depressed mood, and help participants identify activities that counter a depressed mood.

Materials

1. Blackboard or whiteboard (with chalk or markers) or flip chart (with markers)
2. HANDOUT 53: Activities
3. HANDOUT 54: Pleasant Activities
4. WORKSHEET 26: Pleasurable Activities (Environment)
5. HOMEWORK 33: A Plan for Changing Environment

Session Content

1. **Review HOMEWORK 32: Anxiety Chains**
2. **Distribute HANDOUT 53: Activities**

    a.   Explain to participants that environments are one of the areas that contribute to depression.
    b.   Explain that people with no plans or scheduled activities may be at higher risk for depression.
    c.   Teach participants that the goal is to either create or go to an environment that will be enjoyable or be a source of satisfaction.
    d.   List potential enjoyable activities on board.

3. **Distribute HANDOUT 54: Pleasant Activities**

   a. Discuss how pleasant activities can be helpful in countering a depressive mood.

      • Have participant's disucss one example of a time a pleasant activity improved their mood.
      • Have participants identify one time they knew their mood would improve if they engaged in a pleasant activity, but did not do so. What was the outcome?

4. **Distribute WORKSHEET 26: Pleasurable Activities (Environment)**
5. **Assign HOMEWORK 33: A Plan for Changing Environment**

Session 9: Changing Habits—Daily Pleasant Activities

Objective

This session will:

1. Introduce skills for developing daily pleasant activities.

The primary objective of this session is to help participants develop a list of daily pleasant activities that will assist in preventing a drift toward negative emotions.

Materials

1. Blackboard or whiteboard (with chalk or markers) or flip chart (with markers)
2. WORKSHEET 27: Long List of Things I Like to Do
3. HANDOUT 55: Breaking Down a Habit
4. HOMEWORK 34: Placing Pleasant Activities Into My Life

Session Content

1. **Review HOMEWORK 33: A Plan for Changing Environments**
2. **Distribute WORKSHEET 27: Long List of Things I Like to Do**

   a. How you feel is partly determined by what you do.
   b. Developing daily pleasant activities helps prevent a drift toward negative emotions.
   c. List on the board reasons participants' have given up doing pleasurable activities.

3. **Distribute HANDOUT 55: Breaking Down a Habit**

   a. A habit involves knowledge, a skill, and desire

    b.   Brainstorm with the group and list all the "yellow" light routines or behaviors that can lead to depression

- e.g., places where drug dealers are, overeating, ignoring others.

    c.   With the group, list alternate behaviors that can replace the routines or behaviors that lead to a depression-related habit.

4.   **Assign HOMEWORK 34: Placing Pleasant Activities Into My Life**

Session 10: Changing Thoughts and Feelings

Objective

This session will:

1.   Teach the participants strategies to change thoughts and feelings.

The primary objective of this session is to discuss with participants the thoughts and feelings that contribute to depression, and to teach participants strategies to change their thoughts and feelings.

Materials

1.   Blackboard or whiteboard (with chalk or markers) or flip chart (with markers)
2.   HANDOUT 56: Thought Stopping Skill
3.   WORKSHEET 28: Categories of Red Thoughts
4.   WORKSHEET 28: My Emotions Relapse Prevention Plan
5.   "Emotions Management" Graduation Certificate
6.   Post-module Quiz

Session Content

1.   **Review and take up HOMEWORK 34: Placing Pleasant Activities Into My Life**
2.   **Discuss the participant's yellow or red thoughts/feelings in their chain toward depression.**

    a.   Emphasize that these can be changed.
    b.   Discuss how participants have successfully changed their thoughts/ feelings in the past.

3.   **HANDOUT 56: Thought Stopping Skill**

    a.   Thought stopping takes practice and discipline.

4. Complete the session exercise

    a. Select a few negative statements from the examples participants gave earlier. Ask participants to close their eyes and listen as you repeat the words. Repeat the statement aloud several times. After about five repetitions, make a loud noise such as a loud clap, and simultaneously yell stop. Then ask participants to describe what they experienced. Their answers will probably be something like, "I couldn't remember the statement you were repeating."

    b. Ask the participants what just happened. Were you able to keep thinking about the statement I was repeating? Did you notice that the loud noise made you stop thinking about anything else? This exercise shows that you can interrupt a repetitive thought, even one that is unpleasant.

    c. Another exercise. This time I will give you a negative statement, and I want you to begin repeating it in your head. When you hear a loud clap, I want YOU to yell stop as loudly and quickly as you can. Now imagine yourself in a situation where you've just had an argument with your best friend. Repeat to yourself, "I'll get even with him. I hate him! I'll get even with him. I hate him! I'll get even with him. I hate him!" (*Clap hands loudly. Participants should yell stop. Ask participants to describe what they experienced.*)

5. **WORKSHEET 28: Categories of Red Thoughts**
6. **WORKSHEET 29: My Emotions Relapse Prevention Plan**
7. **"Emotions Management" Graduation Certificate**
8. **Post-module Quiz**

19 Module VII
Associates

This treatment module employs social-cognitive learning theory as the theoretical underpinning to explain and change antisocial behavior. Consistent with social-cognitive learning theory, our thoughts and feelings, our habits (past behavioral repertoire), and our environment interact to contribute to our behavior. Our associates provide the social support (reinforcement) for the expression of our behavior and attitudes. The group process therefore seeks to identify and change the social reinforcement that results in CJ-PMI's behavior. We have developed a model that we use with the CJ-PMIs that incorporates these four influences (thoughts/feelings, habits, environment and associates) called the Circle of Change. Through the use of this model we demonstrate for the participant how these four influences have brought him to where he is today and how they can be used to his advantage and help him achieve his life goals (success).

The "Associates" module focuses on building the motivation to change, on creating and maintaining prosocial relationships, on distancing participants from their current criminal associations, and on THE Associates Plan for building a prosocial network which is their relapse prevention plan.

Building the motivation to change is found by exploring the participants' life goals. Among their life goals is their desire to get out of and stay out of jail along with job or family aspirations. Most participants do identify the goal of remaining crime-free as their first priority. Once the participant goals have been established, the Circle of Change is introduced as the model to explain their behavior. Initially, both positive and negative behavior is reviewed within the model. The participants begin to see the model and intervention as a positive approach (meeting their goals) rather than a negative approach that gets them to stop doing something. Participants often deny the influence of others on their life as it is perceived as a threat to their ego and autonomy. Therefore, the model shows the pervasive influence of social peers on behavior. Once participants can recognize the influence of social relationships on behavior, then an exploration of their past relationships is undertaken. This exploration reveals many individuals who have provided the social support for antisocial behavior and are individuals who are not consistent with their stated goals. This allows the participant to arrive at his or her own conclusion that he or she needs to change his or her associates.

Next this module focuses on creating and maintaining prosocial relationships. Included in this section are sessions that include the cognitive restructuring of defeating thoughts, linking thought and behavior, identifying high likelihood places for meeting positive individuals, managing the anxious feelings associated with new and unfamiliar experiences, the nitty-gritty "how-tos" of meeting new people and making small talk, developing a plan of action, and evaluating new relationships. All of these areas of intervention are related the guiding model, the Circle of Change.

Participants then develop a plan for meeting new people, specifically people who will advance their goal of remaining crime-free. The same techniques can also be used to advance their personal employment or educational goals. Plans for meeting people include "locations of high likelihood." Locations of high likelihood are places where the participant is most likely to find people with shared prosocial interests. These most often involve leisure activities, so participants are encouraged to use their leisure interests as a springboard for meeting prosocial others.

The module provides strategies for distancing the CJ-PMI from antisocial others. These include consideration of living arrangements, employment opportunities, and accounting for all of their time in prosocial pursuits. Difficult issues such as what to do when you have a criminal family member are addressed. How does one avoid a brother or cousin who is involved with crime and still maintain family relationships that may be quite positive?

Finally the module helps the participant develop "THE Associates Plan" (relapse prevention plan). This includes designing a plan that includes both the positive movement toward prosocial others and the withdrawal from antisocial others. Other aspects of the plan include the voluntary accountability from a prosocial mentor as well as working with supervising authorities. Having significant others aware of this plan is seen as essential to the participants' long-term success.

The Circle of Change is an adaptation from Bandura's triadic reciprocity model for explaining behavior. Within therapeutic contexts a similar model is the ABC model (antecedents, behavior, consequences). The Circle of Change model is somewhat different in that it is visual, and as you will see in the subsequent version, contains decision points and pictorially represents movement toward life goals or the status quo, which has a motivational component. The aim of the Circle of Change model is to be adaptable to multiple treatment targets. For example, while this module focuses on associates, the Circle of Change could just as easily be adapted to the treatment target of substance abuse, emotions management, or criminal cognitions/attitudes.

The Circle of Change

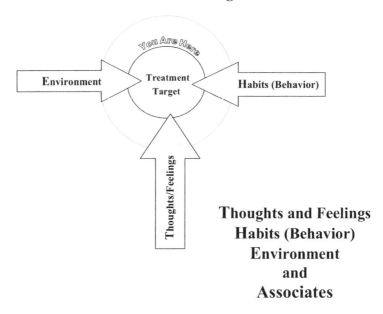

Figure 20.1 Circle of Change

Environment can be either external or internal states. For example hunger pangs are "internal" to the person but definitely a part of their environment. Also, proximity to fast food restaurants are also a part of the person's "external" environment. What the person thinks and feels (thoughts and feelings) about these two environmental stimuli will interact with their past behavior (habits) and together will direct their behavior. Someone who is choosing to lose weight or eat a more healthy diet can make some changes to their environment (i.e., food sources) but not others (i.e., hunger pangs). Pivotal to the change process are the thoughts, feelings, and habits that require change. The presence of the "you are here" and "life goals" visually demonstrates to the participant that change and goal attainment are achieved through the development of new behavior habits.

Content

The "Associates" module includes 10 sessions to help participants identify negative social influences, develop social skills, and build a prosocial network of associates.

Session 1 introduces the participant to how thoughts, habits, and environment influence behavior, with a specific focus on associates.

Session 2 helps the participant explore their own relationships, both past and present, and the influences these relationships have had upon them.

Session 3 further explores the influence of relationships and how they have helped or hindered the participant in meeting life goals.

Session 4 introduces the participant to how their thoughts and feelings influence their behavior.

Session 5 helps the participant identify potential negative or anxious thoughts that may impede their development of new associations.

Session 6 further develops the management of negative thoughts and introduces the participant to the basics of social skills.

Session 7 introduces the participant to "places of high likelihood" for meeting either criminal or prosocial people and introduces the development of productive leisure time.

Session 8 introduces the participant to the stoplight heuristic when evaluating potential new relationships.

Session 9 assists the participant to develop a plan for prosocial networks that will help them meet life goals.

Session 10 is the final session that is designed to help participants refine their plan for development of prosocial networks based upon the skills and strategies introduced in the module.

Treatment Process

Conceptually, the mechanism of change for treating criminal attitudes, substance abuse, or thinking deficits is different than the "Associates" treatment module for criminal associations. The former rely upon changing and maintaining change within the individual. For example, changing an attitude requires the participant to change their evaluation of crime. This will involve cognitive restructuring, insight, and a conscious desire of the individual to challenge the status quo attitude on an ongoing basis. Successfully changing antisocial associations involves changing the external stimuli and experiences of the participant and relying upon those external changes (prosocial individuals) to influence the internal change on an ongoing basis. In other words to allow the same processes that brought and sustained the participant in antisocial behavior to lead and sustain him or her in prosocial pursuits.

Treatment Goals

The overarching treatment goals of the "Associates" module are that participants will:

1. Identify negative social influences that support criminal behavior and impede recovery
2. Build skills necessary to foster prosocial relationships
3. Develop a plan to build a prosocial network of associates.

Session 1: Exploring the Influences of Others

Objective

This session will:

1. Explore the thoughts, habits, and environments that have led the participant to where he is now
2. Introduce the main sources of our behavior and then specifically explore the social influences that led us to where we are within the context of the Circle of Change.

The primary objective of this session is to introduce in neutral terms (examples using non-criminal behavior) those social-cognitive influences that have contributed to our behavior and how we got where we are.

Materials

1. Blackboard or whiteboard (with chalk or markers) or flip chart (with markers)
2. Pre-module Quiz
3. HANDOUT 57: THE Associates Circle of Influence
4. WORKSHEET 30: Case Study—Joan MacDonald
5. HOMEWORK 35: The Circle of Change: Thoughts, Habits, and Environment

Session Content

1. Remind participants of their goals from the mental illness sessions and that this module examines how associates help or hinder the achievement of those goals.
2. Distribute HANDOUT 57: THE Associates Circle of Influence, which is a modified version of Albert Bandura's model of behavior.

   a. Focus on the first triad. Use examples to illustrate how thoughts, habits, and environment have led us to where we are in our lives today.
   b. Emphasize that these three influences are interrelated and can result in a cycle that prevents you from moving forward.

3. Now focus on the second triad. Reiterate that three areas of our functioning influence us: (a) our thoughts and feelings, (b) our habits (behavior), and (c) our environment. Each area is supported by those with whom we spend time (associates).

   a. Be prepared with a POSITIVE example. The facilitator should find out information on someone who is well-known (popular; e.g., Taylor Swift). Ask the participants what they think that Taylor

Swift's habits are, what her thoughts are about life, and how she feels about music. Where does she spend much of her time and with whom does she likely spend much of her time? What influence do they think her thoughts have on her behavior, or what influence do they think her associates have on her behavior?

b. Take time to use at least two positive role models as examples.

4. **Distribute WORKSHEET 30: Case Study—Joan MacDonald**

a. These three areas influence us directly and are influenced by whom we associate with. Let's examine a case study and determine how associates can influence thoughts, habits, and environment.

5. **Assign HOMEWORK 35: The Circle of Change: Thoughts, Habits, and Environment**

a. Inform participants that we have demonstrated that our friends influence our thoughts, our habits, and our environment. Our thoughts, habits and environment can then influence WHAT WE DO (our behavior). For instance, committing a crime is a behavior. They are to work through three examples for homework.

Session 2: Exploring My Relationships

Objective

This session will:

1. Explore relationships that have been part of the participants' lives in the past, and relationships that are part of their current life.

The primary objective of this session is to help the participant explore their relationships, both past and present, and the influences these relationships have had upon them.

Materials

1. Blackboard or whiteboard (with chalk or markers) or flip chart (with markers)
2. HANDOUT 58: Case Study—Frederick Chapman
3. WORKSHEET 31: Exploring Frederick's Relationships
4. HOMEWORK 36: Relationship Activities Inventory

Session Content

1. **Review HOMEWORK 35: The Circle of Change: Thoughts, Habits, and Environments**

2. Define "relationship"—a relationship is a connection we have with another person.

   a. Explain that not all relationships are the same.

      - i.e. we can have relationships that involve reciprocity (give and take) such as romantic relationships and friendships. We can have one-way relationships such as professional relationships. We can have relationships that involve responsibility such as parental or caregiver.

   b. Discuss what kinds of things you do in a relationship?

      - Activities such as family, work and social activities. "Are all activities positive?" Consider substance abuse and idle time.

3. **Distribute HANDOUT 58: Case Study—Frederick Chapman**
4. **Distribute WORKSHEET 31: Exploring Frederick's Relationships**
5. **Assign HOMEWORK 36: Relationship Activities Inventory**

   a. Draw the participants' attention to the three portions of the assignment. Outline that they are to consider people from three different times in their lives (childhood, teen, adulthood).
   b. Note, if the participant came to prison in their late teens, then have them complete the adult associates section and omit the teenage section.
   c. Advise participants not to complete the fourth and fifth columns of the assignment. We revisit those columns in later sessions.

Session 3: Evaluating Relationships

Objective

This session will:

1. Assist the participant in evaluating relationships from their past and current life, and identify how those people influenced them.

The primary objective of this session is to explore with participants the influence of relationships and how they have helped or hindered the participant in meeting life goals.

Materials

1. Blackboard or whiteboard (with chalk or markers) or flip chart (with markers)
2. Red and green stickers

3. HANDOUT 59: Conclusions From the Relationship and Activities Inventory
4. HANDOUT 60: How I Learn and Motivation for Associations
5. HOMEWORK 37: Evaluating What I Learned From the Red Dot Relationships

Session Content

1. **Review The Circle of Change from Session 2 using the diagram of the overall program.**

   a. Prompt participants to start to think about what they learn from their associates.

2. **Review HOMEWORK 36: My Relationships and Activities Inventory**

   a. Have participants share examples from their past and current lives.
   b. Remind participants they do not have to give their associates' real names.
   c. Look for patterns that indicate a growing away from family influences to the influences of antisocial others.
   d. Ask participants to identify how individuals in their lives responded or reacted to their mental illness. Which people were helpful and which people were not helpful? Look for people who encouraged the mentally ill to abuse alcohol and drugs.
   e. Provide each participant with red and green stickers. Have the participants place a red sticker beside those with criminal behavior or people who were not helpful to them in managing their symptoms of mental illness. Then place a green sticker beside those without criminal behavior.

      • Ask the question—**Where are they (the red sticker people) now? Be prepared for the fact that some of them have died.**

3. **Distribute HANDOUT 59: Conclusions From the Relationship and Activities Inventory**

   a. Ask the question—**What did you learn from the red dot relationships?**
   b. Have participants share examples of what they learned. For example, substance use, stealing, dishonesty, getting away with things, etc.
   c. Look for repetition in answers, and point out to group members that once you learn a new behavior, it is often reinforced by others. For example, if you learned to get away with stealing small items, perhaps another friend reinforced this behavior by stealing large items with more monetary value. The stealing behaviors are being reinforced.

4. **Distribute HANDOUT 60: How I Learn and Motivation for Associations**

   a. Teach "How We Learn" through asking the participants, "How do we learn from other people?" Try to elicit the four responses on the handout.
   b. Teach "Motivations for Associations" through asking the participants, "What motivates you to associate with someone?" "Why do you spend time with certain people? What do you get out of it?" Try to elicit the four responses on the handout.

5. **Assign HOMEWORK 37: Evaluating What I Learned From the Red Dot Relationships**

   a. Indicate to participants that they are to list their red dot relationships and identify what they learned from each person.

Session 4: Thoughts, Feelings, and Behavior

Objective

This session will:

1. Assist the participant in identifying how their thoughts about a certain situation can affect how they behave.

The primary objective of this session is to introduce the role cognitions (thoughts) play in directing our behavior. Other programs may use the ABC model, but we use the Circle of Change to demonstrate the principles of the cognitive influences on behavior.

Materials

1. Blackboard or whiteboard (with chalk or markers) or flip chart (with markers)
2. HANDOUT 61: Thoughts, Feelings and Changing Directions
3. WORKSHEET 32: The Relationship Between Thought and Action—Jack's Problems
4. WORKSHEET 33: The Relationship Between Thought and Action
5. HOMEWORK 38: My Thought and Action Experience

Session Content

1. **Review HOMEWORK 37: Evaluating What I Learned From the Red Dot Relationships**

2. **Distribute HANDOUT 61: Thoughts, Feelings and Changing Directions**

   a. Use an example situation and write it on the board with class participation.
   b. Demonstrate how different thoughts about an event can result in different actions.

3. **Distribute WORKSHEET 32: The Relationship Between Thought and Action—Jack's Problems**
4. **Distribute WORKSHEET 33: The Relationship Between Thought and Action**

   a. Have the participants work in small groups.

5. **Assign HOMEWORK 38: My Thought and Action Experience**

   a. Indicate to participants that they are to now choose a real-life situation and state what they thought about the event and what they did. Then, they are to identify two alternative thoughts and actions.

Session 5: Exploring Thoughts About Creating New Relationships and Managing Anxiety

Objective

This session will:

1. Explore some negative thoughts the participants may have about meeting new people and maintaining new relationships.

The primary objective of this session is to help the participant identify potential negative or anxious thoughts that may impede their development of new prosocial associations.

Materials

1. Blackboard or whiteboard (with chalk or markers) or flip chart (with markers)
2. WORKSHEET 34: Possible Stumbling Blocks to Creating New Prosocial Relationships
3. HOMEWORK 39: Replacing My Negative Thoughts
4. WORKSHEET 35: Anxious Situations and Their Management—Situation #1
5. HOMEWORK 40: Anxious Situations and Their Management—Situation #2

Session Content

1. Review HOMEWORK 38: My Thought and Action Experience.
2. Remind the participants of the Circle of Change and the influence of environment on your thoughts and feelings.
3. Distribute WORKSHEET 34: Possible Stumbling Blocks to Creating New Prosocial Relationships.

   a. Draw the participants' attention to the different obstacles they may encounter when trying to meet new people.
   b. Ask the participants to identify the negative thoughts they may have when faced with these obstacles.
   c. If the participants struggle, offer examples. For instance, for the obstacle of being labeled, negative thoughts may include "no one will give me a chance" and "everyone is judging me."
   d. Take on a couple of the negative thoughts given and have the participants offer positive replacement thoughts.

4. Assign HOMEWORK 39: Replacing My Negative Thoughts

   a. Inform participants that they are to identify five negative thoughts they have about creating new relationships in their lives. For each negative thought they are to identify two positive replacement thoughts.

5. Explain that another purpose of this session is to build on the cognition-behavior link by identifying a specific cognition, anxiety (fear, apprehension), and spend time showing participants how to minimize and control anxious thoughts.

   a. Write on the board or flip chart "anxiety" and related words such as apprehension, uncertain, fear, worried, nervous, etc.

6. Review the management of anxiety specifically as it relates to meeting new people, and specifically, people who are not accepting of criminal behavior.
7. Distribute WORKSHEET 35: Anxious Situations and Their Management—Situation #1
8. Distribute HOMEWORK 40: Anxious Situations and Their Management—Situation #2

Session 6: First Steps to Positive Relationships

Objective

This session will:

1. Introduce the participant to the first steps to creating new positive relationships.

The primary objective of this session is to educate the participants that anxiety in social situations is often because we are not quite sure what to do. It is in this session that we begin the process of teaching the participants the basics of meeting new people and making small talk.

Materials

1. Blackboard or whiteboard (with chalk or markers) or flip chart (with markers)
2. HANDOUT 62: READY, 1, 2, 3
3. HOMEWORK 41: Developing Our Go-To Conversation Starters

Session Content

1. Review HOMEWORK 39: Replacing My Negative Thoughts and HOMEWORK 40: Anxious Situations and Their Management—Situation #2

   a. While taking up the homework, look for and comment on any ideas of not knowing how to act or what to do in social situations.

2. Normalize social anxiety for participants—we all get socially nervous from time to time. Explain that skills to cope with social anxiety can be developed. Note that, in fact, many successful people such as politicians and presidents of large companies hire people to teach them what to do and say in social situations.

3. Distribute HANDOUT 62: READY, 1, 2, 3 for making small talk.

   a. READY—preparation
   b. 1—Approach the person and introduce yourself
   c. 2—Communication and the art of small talk
   d. 3—Wrap up and leave with an opening.

4. Get a participant volunteer and create a scenario where the Counselor demonstrates the Ready, 1, 2, 3

5. Provide HOMEWORK 41: Developing Our Go-To Conversation Starters

Session 7: First Steps to Positive Relationships and Role-Play and Identifying Places of High Likelihood

Objective

This session will:

1. Review and practice the steps in making the first contact with a new person

2. Assist the participant in recognizing the places of high likelihood (PHL) for meeting criminal associates and PHL of meeting new pro-social people
3. Assist participants in recognizing the importance of using leisure time to meet life goals.

The primary objective of this session is to introduce to participants "places of high likelihood" for meeting either criminal or prosocial people and introduces the development of productive leisure time.

Materials

1. Blackboard or whiteboard (with chalk or markers) or flip chart (with markers)
2. Content Quiz
3. WORKSHEET 37: Ready 1, 2, 3
4. HANDOUT 63: Time Use and Crime and Planning for Leisure Activities
5. WORKSHEET 36: Places of High Likelihood
6. WORKSHEET 38: Planning for Leisure Activities
7. HOMEWORK 42: Identifying Social Situations
8. HOMEWORK 43: Places of High Likelihood

Session Content

1. Review HOMEWORK 41: Developing Our Go-To Conversation Starters
2. Review the READY, 1, 2, 3 heuristic.

   a. See if the group can remember the steps without referring to their notes.

3. Distribute and discuss WORKSHEET 37: Ready 1, 2,3

Therapist Note: Have one or two participants practice the skills on you (the therapist) with the help and encouragement of the class.

---

4. Create a scenario and have the participants practice their skills on each other
5. Distribute WORKSHEET 36: Places of High Likelihood.

   a. This session introduces the idea that locations (ENVIRON-MENT) determine the type of people that we will meet who will have either positive or negative influences on our behavior. Refer back to THE Associates model. Past environments have been places of high likelihood (PHL) for locating antisocial people.

b. Use THE Associates model to explain how environment can influence your thoughts and behavior.

c. Use the example of their antisocial past. Have the participants complete the worksheet and emphasize that consequences can be both negative and positive. They will likely be able to identify positive short-term consequences, but it's highly unlikely they will find any positive long-term consequences of returning to PHL of meeting criminal associates.

d. Provide some examples of PHL, such as where would you go if you had an interest in playing guitar, basketball, or computers. Emphasize that these PHL are likely to assist you in meeting new prosocial people. This new environment will influence you in a positive manner as opposed to the old environments.

6. Distribute HANDOUT 63: Time Use and Crime and Planning for Leisure Activities

a. Introduce the use of leisure time to advance prosocial contacts and develop prosocial networks.

b. Define "leisure time." Try to elicit the following response: leisure time is a period of unstructured time, outside of work or obligation, where you do something you enjoy. You voluntarily engage in an activity.

c. Get the group to help you calculate the "leisure time math." Start with how many hours a week devoted to work (include travel time), how many hours to personal issues (hygiene, cooking, chores around the house), how many hours for sleep, then add them up and subtract from 168 (# of hours in the week) and that is your leisure time. Can you get into trouble in that amount of time?

d. Emphasize that we need to account for all of our hours, and that there needs to be a purpose for those hours—this will be important when we run into old acquaintances because we will have something constructive to do instead of just hanging around.

e. What is the purpose of leisure time? To relax, to achieve balance in your life, to advance your hobbies, to spend time doing something you enjoy.

f. Ask: what are some positive leisure activities and some negative leisure activities?

g. Emphasize in Step 1: there is a difference between a hobby and a job. We are fortunate if we enjoy our jobs, but it is necessary to develop interests that are not related to what we do for a living.

h. Emphasize in Step 2: consider activities that are social. For example: if you enjoy working out, consider joining a class or club that fits your interest. If you enjoy going to the movies, consider a movie club or taking a community college course in arts or film. If most of your interests are solitary, consider how they can become more social activities. That is why we are here: to assist you with skills to create new relationships.

7. Distribute WORKSHEET 38: Planning for Leisure Activities

a. Have participants brainstorm positive leisure activities they can do. List positive consequences of developing these activities.

8. Assign HOMEWORK 42: Identifying Social Situations

a. Now participants are to choose two activities and outline a plan to implement these activities upon release.

9. Assign HOMEWORK 43: Places of High Likelihood

a. Participants are to now list places that are likely to influence them in a positive way.

Session 8: Evaluating Potential New Relationships and Creating Distance From Former Criminal Associates

Objective

This session will:

1. Introduce a method for evaluating potential new relationships
2. Learn strategies to create distance with former and future criminal associates.

The primary objective of this session is to learn to create distance between the participant and antisocial others. This includes those antisocial others that he or she already knows and those s/he can potentially meet. The focus here is to show participants that they must evaluate everyone that they meet. This evaluation is a judgment of whether or not that person engages in behavior that will help or hinder the participant. Judgment does not mean condemning the other person.

Materials

1. Blackboard or whiteboard (with chalk or markers) or flip chart (with markers)

2. HANDOUT 64: Evaluating New Relationships
3. HANDOUT 65: Creating Distance With Antisocial Others
4. WORKSHEET 39: Evaluating Potential Relationships
5. HOMEWORK 44: Relationship Scenarios
6. HOMEWORK 45: Your Plan to Create Distance With Antisocial Others

Session Content

1. Review HOMEWORK 42: Identifying Social Situations
2. Take up HOMEWORK 43: Places of High Likelihood that will help meet my goals
3. Review WORKSHEET 38: Planning for Leisure Activities
4. Distribute HANDOUT 64: Evaluating New Relationships
5. Distribute HANDOUT 65: Creating Distance With Antisocial Others
6. Distribute WORKSHEET 39: Evaluating Potential Relationships

   a. Reintroduce the stoplight heuristic. Remind the participants that they evaluated their past relationships using the red/green stickers and that they will now evaluate everyone new that they meet using the same approach.
   b. Red indicates the person has a criminal record OR is involved in criminal activities.
   c. Yellow means you are not sure but there are indications that not everything they do is on the level (yellow means red is coming).
   d. Green means the person does not have a criminal record and is in all points prosocial.
   e. What is the problem with a neutral relationship or a neutral activity? Neutral (yellow) means red is coming.
   f. Discuss strategies to create distance between the participant and both former and possibly future criminal associates.

      • Strategies include:

         o Structured activities—account for all of your time
         o Avoid the old haunts
         o Physically move if you have to
         o Be accountable to someone else for where you go and what you do
         o Manage your time with antisocial family members. If a family member is criminally involved (brother, cousin, etc.) do not be alone with them without a prosocial family member present.

7. Assign HOMEWORK 44: Relationship Scenarios
8. Assign HOMEWORK 45: Your Plan to Create Distance With Antisocial Others

Session 9: Development of the Associates Plan

Objective

This session will:

1. Introduce your plan for success.

The primary objective of this session is for the participant to review the material and create their plan for success.

Materials

1. Blackboard or whiteboard (with chalk or markers) or flip chart (with markers)
2. HANDOUT 66: My Plan to Implement THE Associates Plan
3. HANDOUT 67: Review: What I Need From This Group to Start My Plan
4. HOMEWORK 46: My Plan for Success

Session Content

1. Review HOMEWORK 44: Relationship Scenarios
2. Take up HOMEWORK 45: Your Plan to Create Distance With Anti-social Others
3. Distribute HANDOUT 66: My Plan to Implement THE Associates Plan
4. Distribute HANDOUT 67: Review: What I Need From this Group to Start My Plan

   a. This will include revisiting their goal statements, identifying those people and activities who will assist them in meeting those goals, developing a leisure plan that supports those goals, identify their red-light people, develop a plan to distance themselves from antisocial others, and develop a plan to implement the plan

   b. Identify what steps the participants will take immediately, over the time between now and release, and following release to implement the plan.

   c. Also today will overview the program and introduce THE Associates Plan and its components.

5. Assign HOMEWORK 46: My Plan for Success

Session 10: Development of the Associates Plan—Part II

Objective

This session will:

1. Review with the participants their plan for success with help from the group. It is meant to "fine tune" the plan, which is the relapse prevention plan of this module.

The primary objective of this session is to help participants refine their plan for developing prosocial networks based upon the skills and strategies introduced in the module.

Materials

1. Blackboard or whiteboard (with chalk or markers) or flip chart (with markers)
2. HANDOUT 66: My Plan to Implement THE Associates Plan
3. HOMEWORK 46: Redistribute this document so that participants can rewrite "My Plan for Success"
4. "Associates" Graduation Certificate
5. Post-module Quiz

Session Content

1. Review HANDOUT 66: My Plan to Implement THE Associates Plan
2. Redistribute a blank copy of HOMEWORK 46, which is the document that participants will use to finalize their plan

   a. This session will be given over to the group's step-by-step review of their plans.
   b. With the feedback and assistance from both the group and facilitator, have each participant review their plan. Provide positive feedback and suggest they consider (this is their plan) feedback.

3. Distribute a second blank copy of HOMEWORK 46: My Plan for Success so that the participant can make a good and final copy
4. Conduct a group feedback session on their overall experience
5. Distribute "Associates" Graduation Certificates
6. Post-module Quiz.

20 Module VIII
Community Skills Development

This module consists of nine sessions designed to provide CJ-PMI with skills to assist them with community reintegration. Specifically, problem solving, communication, and vocational skills are taught in this module. Therapists will model effective problem-solving and communication skills, and participants will be required to practice these skills both in in-group and out-of-group work. It is anticipated that the development of these skills will help the CJ-PMI as they transition out of correctional or forensic settings into community placements and result in improved outcomes including reduced criminal and psychiatric recidivism (e.g., absence of imprisonment, fewer jail days, fewer hospital days, improved psychosocial functioning—more good days).

Content

The "Community Skills Development" module includes nine sessions to educate participants about mental illness, symptoms associated with mental illness, symptoms of criminalness, mechanisms for seeking help, and relapse prevention strategies.

Session 1 provides an overview of the module and teaches participants the importance of effective problem-solving skills. This module also exposes participants to the five steps to effective problem solving that are taught in subsequent sessions.

Sessions 2–4 teach participants the five steps to effective problem solving, with practice of this strategy for solving their common, everyday problems.

Session 5 educates participants about effective communication skills and help them identify their communication skill deficits.

Sessions 6–7 teach and provide opportunities for participants to practice effective communication skills.

Session 8 helps participants identify their job skills and their career interests and values.

Session 9 challenges participants to accept responsibility for past choices, including using crime as a means of supporting oneself. Participants will be educated on effective job and house seeking strategies.

Treatment Process

The "Community Skills Development" module utilizes cognitive-behavioral and social learning theory to help participants gain understanding of their skill deficits and to develop problem-solving, communication, and career skills. The overarching goal of the module is skill development. Thus, the mechanism of change in this module is didactic, with modeling by the therapist to help participants recognize effective use of taught skills. Behavioral practice and repetition will be used extensively to enhance skill development.

Treatment Goals

The goals of the "Community Skills Development" module are that participants will:

1. Learn and demonstrate competence in the five steps to effective problem-solving strategy taught in this module
2. Develop effective communication skills
3. Enhance participant's job and house hunting skills, as well as help them identify their career interests.

Session 1: Problem Solving: What It Is and Why It Is Important

Objective

This session will:

1. Complete pre-testing
2. Review group rules
3. Review participants' personal goals
4. Introduce the "Community Skills Development" module
5. Discuss the THE Skill Development model
6. Help participants begin to recognize how their mental illness and criminalness impacts their ability to problem solve; and how poor problem-solving skills can lead to poor mental health.

The primary objectives of this session are to educate participants about what problem solving is, the importance of developing effective problem-solving strategies, and to help them identify the ways in which they have dealt with problems in the past.

Materials

1. Blackboard or whiteboard (with chalk or markers) or flip chart (with markers)

2. HANDOUT 68 What Is Problem Solving and Why Is It Important?
3. WORKSHEET 39: Your Mental Illness, Criminalness, and Problem Solving
4. WORKSHEET 40: THE Skill Development Model—Your RED Thoughts, Habits, Environments
5. HOMEWORK 47: How Have I Solved My Problems in the Past?
6. Pre-module Quiz

Session Content

1. **Complete Pre-Module Quiz**
2. **Review participant's personal goals**

   a. Each participant reviews their personal goals aloud to the group.

3. **Teach participants about what problem solving is and why it is important**

   a. Distribute HANDOUT 68: What Is Problem Solving and Why Is It Important?

   • Educate participants about what problems and solutions are

     o Begin to normalize how everyone experiences problems
     o Briefly introduce them to the five steps. This will be further discussed in Session 2.

   • Take time to emphasize the impact deficits in problem-solving skills can have on their mental illness

     o Sell them on the benefits of effective problem solving.

4. **Distribute WORKSHEET 39: Your Mental Illness, Criminalness, and Problem Solving**

   a. Have participants complete worksheet individually
   b. Have the participants go around and share their responses
   c. Point out how different symptoms can impact their ability to solve problems

   • Difficulty concentrating and coming up with possible solutions
   • Racing thoughts
   • Distractibility
   • Negative thinking errors, as discussed in Module V
   • Anxiety—fearful of choosing wrong solution, may lead to avoidance behaviors.

   d. Point out how not effectively solving problems can contribute to increase in symptoms

   • Feel more depressed
   • Feel inadequate
   • Feel helpless/hopeless

- More anxiety
- Withdraw from others
- Use substances to deal with problems.

e. Explain how criminalness is involved

- Avoiding problems or self-medicating to reduce impact of problems is irresponsible
- Emphasize this module will teach them strategies to effectively solve problems, so they won't have to avoid or self-medicate.

5. **Distribute WORKSHEET 40: THE Skill Development Model—Your RED Thoughts, Habits, Environments**

a. Have participants complete worksheet individually
b. Have participants share their responses
c. Encourage participants to think about how they have attempted to solve problems in the past

- What negative thoughts and behaviors did they exhibit that made problem solving difficult and ineffective?
- In what situations is it most difficult for them to solve their problems?

6. **Assign HOMEWORK 47: How Have I Solved My Problems in the Past?**

Session 2: The Five Stages to Effectively Solve Problems

Objective

This session will:

1. Educate participants on the five steps to effective problem solving
2. Assist participants in changing their RED thoughts, habits, and environments to GREEN
3. Allow participants to begin practicing the five steps.

The primary objectives of this session are to educate participants about the five stages to problem solving, to assist participants to alter their RED thoughts, habits, and environments to GREEN, to help to change their negative, unrealistic view of problems, and to have participants begin to practice these five stages.

Materials

1. Blackboard or whiteboard (with chalk or markers) or flip chart (with markers)

2. HANDOUT 69: Five Stages of Problem Solving
3. WORKSHEET 41: The Five-Stage Problem-Solving Worksheet
4. WORKSHEET 42: Changing From RED to GREEN
5. WORKSHEET 43: Learning to Use the Five Stages of Problem Solving
6. HOMEWORK 48: Practicing the Five Stages

Session Content

1. **Review HOMEWORK 47: How Have I Solved My Problems in the Past?**

    a. Be sure to have the participants talk about their old ways of problem solving, and how effective they have been in the past.
    b. Discuss where each participant needs improvement.

2. **Educate participants on the five stages of problem solving**

    a. Distribute HANDOUT 69: Five Stages of Problem Solving
    b. Be sure to spend enough time thoroughly explaining each stage

    •   When explaining the problem orientation, point out the RED thoughts they identified in the previous sessions, and how these thoughts need to be changed in order to be able to effectively move through the stages and solve their problems.

3. **Assist participants in changing their self-identified RED thoughts, habits, and environments to GREEN**

    a. Distribute WORKSHEET 42: Changing From RED to GREEN
    b. It's important for participants to begin to accept problems are a part of life, and do not need to be viewed as threatening situations that are to be avoided.

3. **Have participants begin to implement the five stages in session**

    a. Distribute WORKSHEET 43: Learning to Use the Five Stages of Problem Solving and WORKSHEET 41: The Five-Stage Problem-Solving Worksheet

    •   Do one problem on the board together to assist participants in becoming familiar with the stages
    •   Have participants then finish the worksheet individually

        o   Review together each participant's responses
        o   Assure participants this may not come easy, but with practice the goal is to make it come naturally.
        o   Identify areas in which participants are having difficulty, and continue to educate and clarify.

4. **Assign HOMEWORK 48: Practicing the Five Stages of Problem Solving**

   a. Be sure to redistribute multiple copies of HANDOUT 69: The Five Stages of Problem Solving to assist participants in completing their homework.

Session 3: Practice Makes Perfect: Continue the Use of the Five Stages

Objective

This session will:

1. Assist participants in identifying the difficulties they have in implementing the five stages
2. Allow participants to continue to practice the five stages, to help build self-efficacy.

The primary objectives of this session are to work through the difficulties the participants have utilizing the five stages, and help identify their areas of improvement, and to continue to practice the five stages to effective problem solving.

Materials

1. Blackboard or whiteboard (with chalk or markers) or flip chart (with markers)
2. HANDOUT 69: The Five Stages of Effective Problem Solving

Session Content

1. **Review HOMEWORK 48: Practicing the Five Stages of Problem Solving**

   a. Have each participant go to the board and write out the five stages for one of the problems they identified and worked through.
   b. Have the group give each member feedback on their efforts.
   c. If a participant was unsuccessful in solving their problem, have the participant, along with the group, identify what may have gone wrong, and as a group rework through the stages.
   d. Have each participant talk about their experience completing the homework.

  e.   Be sure to give praise for their efforts, and work toward building their self-efficacy.

2.   **Reassign HOMEWORK 48: Practicing the Five Stages**

  a.   Again, be sure to redistribute multiple copies of HANDOUT 69: The Five Stages to Effective Problem Solving to assist participants in completing their homework.
  b.   Encourage the participants to begin to identify and work through problems they anticipate upon release.

Session 4: Overlearning the Five Stages

Objective

This session will:

1.   Allow participants to continue to practice the five stages
2.   To help participants build self-efficacy in problem solving.

The primary objective of this session is to have participants overlearn the five stages of effective problem solving.

Materials

1.   Blackboard or whiteboard (with chalk or markers) or flip chart (with markers)

Session Content

1.   **Review HOMEWORK 48: Practicing the Five Stages**

  a.   Have each participant go to the board and write out the five stages for one of the problems they identified and worked through.
  b.   Have the group give each member feedback on their efforts.
  c.   If a participant was unsuccessful in solving their problem, have the participant, along with the group, identify what may have gone wrong, and as a group rework through the stages.
  d.   Have each participant talk about their experience completing the homework.
  e.   Be sure to give praise for their efforts, and work toward building their self-efficacy.

Session 5: The Basics of Interpersonal Communication

Objective

This session will:

1. Educate participants on the various skills involved in effective communication
2. Assist participants in identifying their problem areas in terms of effective communication.

The primary objectives of this session are to educate participants about the multiple components of effective communication skills, as well as help them identify where their communication skill deficits lie.

Materials

1. Blackboard or whiteboard (with chalk or markers) or flip chart (with markers)
2. HANDOUT 70: The Communication Process
3. HANDOUT 71: The Importance of Nonverbal Communication
4. HANDOUT 72: Listening a MUST for Effective Communication
5. HOMEWORK 49: My Difficulties With Communication Checklist
6. HOMEWORK 50: My Observations of Others

Session Content

1. **Educate participants about the basics of communication**

   a. Distribute HANDOUT 70: The Communication Process
   b. When discussing the five basic social skills, point out how certain mental illnesses can lead to deficits in this area, particularly those diagnosed with schizophrenia.

2. **Educate participants about nonverbal communication**

   a. Distribute HANDOUT 71: The Importance of Nonverbal Communication

3. **Educate participants about listening skills**

   a. Distribute HANDOUT 72: Listening a MUST for Effective Communication
   b. Have participants identify the roadblocks they encounter when trying to listen to others.

     c.   Provide feedback on the participants' communication styles when they are interacting with the other group members and the group leader.

4. **Assign HOMEWORK 49: My Difficulties With Communication Checklist**

     a.   It is important for the participants to review the handouts and identify specific areas that they struggle with. This will help you to tailor the next two sessions to the specific needs of the participants.

5. **Assign HOMEWORK 50: My Observations of Others**

     a.   Have the participants observe others communicating. They should attempt to identify the nonverbal gestures, the listening skills employed, how effective the sender was at sending the message, and how effective the receiver was at receiving the message. Have them note what went well and what went wrong in the communication process.

Session 6: Practicing Social Skills—Using Modeling and Role Plays

Objective

This session will:

1. Allow participants to observe appropriate and effective communication techniques in session
2. Have participants begin practicing effective communication.

The primary objectives of this session are for the therapists to model effective communication techniques and to allow participants to practice these techniques, so participants will become comfortable with these tools and add them into their repertoire.

Materials

1. Blackboard or whiteboard (with chalk or markers) or flip chart (with markers)
2. WORKSHEET 46: Role Play Notes
3. HOMEWORK 51: Using the Skills I Practiced

Session Content

1. **Review HOMEWORK 49: My Difficulties With Communication**

   a. It is important for participants to be specific about areas of improvement. This will allow you to tailor the role plays to each participant's needs.

      • For those with limited insight it will be important for you to help identify those areas. This exercise may be particularly difficult for those suffering from schizophrenia.

2. **Review HOMEWORK 50: My Observation of Others**

   a. Have each participant share their observation of others.
   b. Be sure to have each participant suggest ways in which an ineffective communication they observed could have been improved.
   c. If the communication they observed was effective and both parties appeared satisfied, be sure to have participants articulate why it was effective.

      • If participants are struggling be sure to help guide them along, and have them refer back to the handouts presented in Session 5.

3. **Distribute WORKSHEET 46: Role Play Notes**

   a. Instruct participants to take notes about what they see during the role plays.
   b. The participants should be taking notes about the nonverbal gestures they observe and the elements of active listening they noticed. They should also be making comments about the effect the communication style has on the sender and receiver. Also, have them note any questions they have about the interaction.

4. **ROLE PLAY 1: Model Basic Communication Skills and Active Listening**

   a. Conduct a role play with a participant in the group.
   b. Have the participant describe a recent *positive* experience
      • Examples: receiving a happy letter from home, receiving GED, promotion at work
   c. You are to be modeling active listening.
      • Be sure you are summarizing what you hear, and reflect back his feelings.
   d. While the role play is being conducted, have each participant watching the interaction take notes on WORKSHEET 42.

5. **Review ROLE PLAY 1 as a group**

   a. Have each participant share their observations
      - Make a list of the participants' observations on the board.

   b. A list should be compiled of all the nonverbal gestures, as well as what the receiver did to communicate they were listening.

      - For those participants with severe deficits it will be important to go over very basic communication skills (e.g., nodding your head, making eye contact, saying "uh-huh" periodically during the interaction).

6. **ROLE PLAY 2: Continue to Model Basic Communication Skills and Active Listening**

   a. Conduct a second role play with a different participant in the group
   b. Have a participant describe a recent *negative* experience

      - Examples: car breaking down, stressed out at work, have not received a letter from home.

   c. Continue to model basic nonverbal gestures and active listening
   d. Continue to have participants take notes using WORKSHEET 42.

7. **Review ROLE PLAY 2 as a group**

   a. Have each participant share their observations

      - Make a list of the participants' observations on the board.

   b. A list should be compiled of all nonverbal gestures, as well as what the receiver did to communicate they were listening.

      - For those participants with severe deficits it will be important to go over very basic communication skills (e.g., nodding your head, making eye contact, saying "uh-huh" periodically during the interaction).

8. **Have participants begin conducting role plays**

   a. The role plays should be tailored to the responses the participants gave on HOMEWORK 50: My Observations of Others. Be sure to match the role play scenario to each participant's needs.
   b. Have two participants conduct a role play in front of the group
   c. The participants in the role play should be practicing the basics of communication and active listening
   d. Participants observing should continue taking notes
   e. Review participants' observations. Be sure you and other group members are providing positive, as well as constructive feedback to those in the role play.

9. Continue, as time permits, to practice role plays until each partici-pant has had the opportunity to be the sender and receiver in the communication exchange.

   a. Again it's important you are matching the role play scenario to the participants' needs
   b. Following is a list of scenarios that may be helpful in having the participants practice the skills from HOMEWORK 50: My Observations of Others.

10. Assign HOMEWORK 51: Using the Skills I Practiced

Role Play Scenarios

Conversation Skills

1. Listening to others: in these role plays participants should be practic-ing making eye contact, nodding head, appropriate posture and body distance, and active listening (i.e., summarizing other's points and reflecting back other's feelings).

   a. Listening to someone talk about receiving a happy letter from home.
   b. Listening to someone talk about their day at work.
   c. Listening to someone talk about a movie they saw.
   d. Listening to a family member tell you about a problem they recently encountered.

2. Starting conversations: in these role plays participants should be practicing judging when and where to begin a conversation, greet-ing others, making small talk, and correctly judging when to end the conversation.

   a. You are at a family BBQ.
   b. You are in the waiting room at the doctor's office.
   c. You are eating lunch with a new coworker.
   d. You are at your children's school function with other parents.

3. Maintaining conversations: in these role plays participants should be practicing asking others general questions, then following up with spe-cific questions. Additionally, it is important for participants to practice judging whether someone is interested in maintaining the conversation. Also, for those participants who have difficulty staying on topic, this role play will provide a good opportunity to practice that skill as well.

   a. Eating lunch with a friend from work.
   b. Talking with your cellmate after their family visit.
   c. At a social gathering with friends.

4. Joining a conversation: in these role plays the participants are to practice recognizing when it is appropriate to join an ongoing conversation, how to join a conversation (e.g., saying "May I join you"), and to stay on topic of the ongoing conversation.

    a. In the chow hall, you see two friends eating and talking.
    b. Two coworkers are talking about your favorite sports team or favorite hobby.
    c. At a BBQ at a friend's house, three individuals are talking about how good the food is.

5. Ending conversations: in these role plays participants should be practicing how to use verbal statements and nonverbal gestures to wrap up a conversation. Additionally, it is important participants learn to end a conversation during an appropriate time (i.e., when the person finishes speaking).

    a. On the phone with a friend or family member.
    b. Bumping into a friend at the supermarket (or while running errands).
    c. Meeting a friend for lunch, but have an appointment immediately following.
    d. Talking with a coworker before your shift starts.

Conflict Management

1. Responding to untrue accusations and leaving stressful situations: Participants are to practice remaining calm and speaking civilly with the other person; requesting the person to stop; getting assistance if necessary; being mindful of their thoughts, feelings, and physiological signs of stress and anger; and appropriately leaving the situation when necessary.

    a. A family member has accused you of stealing money.
    b. Your partner accuses you of not doing your household chores.
    c. A correctional officer accuses you of starting a fight.
    d. A friend accuses you of cheating in a game.

Assertiveness

1. Making requests: in these role plays, participants should be practicing how to be polite, but direct, and to be clear and specific in their requests. It may help for participants to communicate how they would feel if the person accepted the request.

    a. Asking a friend to lunch.
    b. Asking a family member/cellmate to turn down the TV while you are working/reading/sleeping.

    c.   Asking a counselor for help with a problem.
    d.   Asking your partner for help with a chore.

2. Refusing requests: in these role plays, participants are to practice speaking politely and calmly, but in a firm and clear manner. They should learn to avoid being rude or hostile.

    a.   A family member asks to borrow money.
    b.   A friend asks for you to go to lunch, but you have a doctor's appointment.
    c.   A family member asks for your help with a yard project, but you had a long day at work.
    d.   A friend asks you to go to a bar, but you are in recovery.

3. Making complaints: in these role plays, participants should practice speaking calmly, but firmly. They should practice stating their complaint in a clear and specific manner, and to suggest solutions to the problem if necessary.

    a.   A family member continues to interrupt you while you are speaking.
    b.   A cashier overcharged you for an item.
    c.   When you receive your paycheck, you realize you were not paid for one day of work.

4. Responding to complaints: in these role plays, participants should practice remaining calm and to actively listen. They should be trying to empathize with the individual and be sure not to be putting up any roadblocks to listening. They should practice summarizing the person's complaint. They should practice taking responsibility without being defensive, and learn to apologize when necessary.

    a.   A family member complains you are interrupting them when they are speaking.
    b.   Your partner complains you are always late.
    c.   Your partner complains you are not helping out enough around the house.
    d.   Your cellmate complains you are playing your music too loud.

5. Expressing negative emotions: in these role plays, participants should practice expressing their negative feelings in a calm but direct manner. Participants should be taught that it is important to express these feelings in order to avoid future arguments or increased negative feelings. Participants should practice being clear on what the person did to upset them, state how it made them feel, and suggest how they can work together to prevent this from happening again.

    a.   Your family has not written you a letter in several weeks.
    b.   You are worried when your partner is out later than expected.

     c. Your counselor/social worker cancels your appointment without informing you.

     d. Your cellmate/roommate/partner left dirty dishes in the sink all week.

6. Expressing anger: although the topic of anger was addressed in Module VI, "Emotions Management," it may be a good idea to readdress some issues the participants may still be struggling with. In these role plays, the emphasis is on expressing anger without hostility. Participants should practice making "I" statements. They should practice speaking calmly, but firmly.

     a. Your friend borrowed a CD, and lost it.

     b. Your cellmate/roommate changes the television channel while you are watching your favorite television show.

     c. A coworker has been slacking on the job, creating more work for you.

7. Making apologies: in these role plays, participants should practice making genuine apologies without minimizing and discounting another's feelings. It is important for participants to practice making direct eye contact, and to assure the person that it won't happen again (if appropriate or realistic).

     a. Taking your stressful day or anger out on a family member.

     b. Attending class/group late.

     c. Interrupting someone while they are talking.

     d. Not paying attention to someone while they are talking.

*For each of these role plays it is important to tailor each scenario to the participant's needs. For higher functioning participants, you may want to combine role plays; for example, combining situations that are stressful, elicit anger, and require the participant to apologize. Also, it may be helpful to ask the participants for situations in which they have had difficulty communicating and use the role play as a way to improve those specific situations.

Session 7: Practice, Practice, Practice: Social Skills Role Plays Continued

Objective

This session will:

1. Allow participants to continue to practice social skills for improved communication with others.

The primary objective of this session is to continue to provide modeling and allowing the participants to practice a variety of skills in a variety of social situations.

Materials

1. Blackboard or whiteboard (with chalk or markers) or flip chart (with markers)
2. WORKSHEET 44: Role Play Notes

Session Content

1. **Review HOMEWORK 51: Using the Skills I Practiced**

   a. Have each participant share the skills they practiced, and have each of them talk about their experience with each skill
   b. Continue to provide feedback to each of the participants, and praise them for their efforts
   c. For participants who encountered difficulties and were unsuccessful in applying the skills, it is important to review the situation with them, ask for feedback from the other participants on what could have been done to improve the communication, and conduct a role play to assist the participant in using that skill.

2. **Continue conducting role plays**

   a. As in Session 6, continue to identify problem areas for the participants and begin practicing those skills
   b. Redistribute WORKSHEET 44: Role Play Notes, and continue to have participants take notes, and provide feedback
   c. If participants find a particular skill difficult, be sure to model that skill first and then redo the role play.

3. **Redistribute HOMEWORK 51: Using the Skills I Practiced**

Session 8: Career Skills, Interests, and Values

Objective

This session will:

1. Allow participants to identify and examine their career skills, interests, and values
2. Have participants develop concrete and realistic career goals

3. Allow participants to identify the barriers to achieving their career goals.

The primary objectives of this session are to have the participants begin identifying the job skills they possess, as well as the career interests and values they hold. Additionally, the participants should begin to identify the existing barriers for participants entering the workforce.

Materials

1. Blackboard or whiteboard (with chalk or markers) or flip chart (with markers)
2. WORKSHEET 45: My Reentry Into the Workforce
3. HOMEWORK 52: My Yellow & RED Thoughts, Habits, and Environments to Finding and Keeping a Prosocial Job

Session Content

1. **Review HOMEWORK 51: Using the Skills I Practiced**

    a. Have each participant share the skills they practiced, and have each of them talk about their experience with each skill
    b. Continue to provide feedback to each of the participants, and praise them for their efforts
    c. For participants who encountered difficulties and were unsuccessful in applying the skills, it is important to review the situation with them, ask for feedback from the other participants on what could have been done to improve the communication, and conduct a role play to assist the participant in using that skill.
    d. In order to bridge the discussion of communication skills and vocational skills, it will be important to point out the importance of communication in the workplace.

        • Discuss the importance of effective communication during interviews
        • Discuss the importance of effective communication among supervisors and coworkers
        • Many jobs require employees to work in teams, thus the skills they have been practicing will be very important in the future.

2. **Distribute WORKSHEET 45: My Reentry Into the Workforce**

    a. Have the participants discuss their current education level, and whether they want to gain more education. It is important to remind participants to set realistic goals, as discussed back in Module I.

    b.   Emphasize to participants the importance of identifying their skills, interests, and values. Have them talk about past employment. What went wrong? Did those jobs not meet their needs?

    c.   Again, emphasize the importance of realistic goals. At this time, have the participants begin talking about the barriers they may face in accomplishing their goals.

- Stigma of being an ex-felon
- Stigma of being mentally ill
- Be up-front about the additional barriers ethnic-minority participants have.

3.   **Distribute HOMEWORK 52: My Yellow & RED Thoughts, Habits, and Environments to Finding and Keeping a Prosocial Job**

Session 9: Finding and Keeping a Job and Housing Issues

Objective

This session will:

1. Have participants identify why they use crime as a means for financial support
2. Educate participants on job seeking and interview skills
3. Educate participants about the importance of housing in recovery.

The primary objectives of this session are to have the participants recognize why they use crime as a means for financial support and the consequences associated with doing so, and to learn to change their negative attitudes about prosocial employment. Participants will be provided with education about how to find and obtain a job. Additionally, participants will be educated about how to seek housing.

Materials

1. Blackboard or whiteboard (with chalk or markers) or flip chart (with markers)
2. HANDOUT 73: How to Find and Interview for a Job
3. HANDOUT 74: Housing for Participants With Mental Illness
4. WORKSHEET 46: Why I Use Crime and Its Consequences
5. WORKSHEET 47: My GREEN Thoughts, Habits, and Environments to Finding & Keeping a Prosocial Job
6. "Community Skills Development" Graduation Certificate
7. Post-module Quiz

Session Content

1. Review HOMEWORK 52: My Yellow & RED Thoughts, Habits, and Environments to Finding and Keeping a Prosocial Job

   a. Have each participant share their responses
   b. Encourage participants to open up about their difficulties in wanting, finding, and keeping a prosocial job
   c. Distribute WORKSHEET 46: Why I Use Crime and Its Consequences

      - Point out criminal thinking styles
      - Many participants, particularly those incarcerated for drug dealing, will have difficulty adjusting to not having the income crime provided. Discuss with the participants the reality of this. Remind participants of their goals, and the consequences of continuing to use crime as a means of financial support.

   d. Distribute WORKSHEET 47: My GREEN Thoughts, Habits, and Environments to Finding and Keeping a Prosocial Job

      - Have each participant share their responses
      - Have the group help participants who have difficulty with this worksheet.

2. Distribute HANDOUT 73: How to Find and Interview for a Job

   a. Educate participants on their legal rights

      - Continue to have participants talk about their fears of not being able to find a job because of their status.

   b. Educate participants on how to find a job (e.g., classifieds, library)
   c. Educate participants on how to interview for a job

      - If time permits, it may be helpful to conduct mock interviews.

3. Distribute HANDOUT 74: Housing for Participants With Mental Illness
4. Distribute "Community Skills Development" Graduation Certificate
5. Post-module Quiz

21 Module IX

Substance Abuse

The aim of this treatment module is to facilitate CJ-PMI understanding, recognizing, and modifying their substance misuse. The principles guiding the "Substance Abuse" treatment module are consistent with principles of psychosocial rehabilitation and the principles of Need and Responsivity from the Risk-Need-Responsivity model of corrections treatment. Consistent with the theoretical orientation of the *CLCO* program, this module incorporates a social-cognitive learning theory with structured exercises (including in and outside of group exercises) to facilitate participant change. In addition, this module incorporates motivational interviewing techniques to facilitate change. By addressing substance abuse within their mental illness, as well as their criminal propensities, participants will be better equipped to utilize skills that will facilitate improved outcomes including reduced criminal and psychiatric recidivism (e.g., absence of imprisonment, fewer jail days, fewer hospital days, improved psychosocial functioning—more good days).

Content

The "Substance Abuse" module includes 10 sessions to educate participants about substance misuse, personal assessment, barriers to change, and strategies needed for change.

Session 1 begins with a motivational interviewing approach that examines the participants' goals within the context of substance abuse. The THE model provides the conceptual framework for change.

Session 2 will assess the participant's levels of substance abuse. Regardless of the level of abuse, the benefit of the module in relation to the participant's goals is emphasized.

Sessions 3 and 4 will educate participants about what is needed to make changes in the area of substance abuse. The THE model and the stoplight analogy are integrated into both sessions.

Session 5 will challenge the participant with seemingly unimportant thoughts/feelings, habits, and environments that move the participant closer to substance misuse, although they may seem unrelated to substance use.

Session 6 will challenge participants on the antecedent thoughts, habits, and environments that lead to substance use.

Session 7 will present refusal skills. Participants will develop and practice substance use refusal skills.

Session 8 will assist the participant in changing and participating in environments that are a source of pleasure and have a green light.

Session 9 will introduce skills for changing habits that are related to substance use.

Session 10 will review the module and create a self-management substance use plan.

Treatment Process

The "Substance Abuse" module utilizes cognitive-behavioral and social learning theory to help participants utilize assessment skills to gain an understanding of their antecedent factors that lead to substance abuse and skills necessary to change their substance abuse patterns. Key skills are refusal skills. The overarching goal of this module is skill development.

Treatment Goals

The overarching treatment goal of the "Substance Abuse" module is participant understanding and the development of skills to reduce the impact of substance use and misuse.

1. Learn the contributors to substance abuse
2. Understand the consequences of substance abuse
3. Develop the skills to reduce substance abuse
4. Develop alternate actions.

Session 1: An Introduction to the Module and Developing Goals

Objective

This session will:

1. Build rapport with the participant
2. Introduce the program and assist the participant in defining his personal life goals
3. Gain permission to continue
4. Help the participant understand the purpose for the intervention.

The primary objective of this session is to introduce to the participant the need for them to define their own life goals and then introduce the idea that the program will show them how to get from here to there.

Materials

1. Blackboard or whiteboard (with chalk or markers) or flip chart (with markers)
2. Pre-module Quiz
3. WORKSHEET 48: Changing My Substance Use Patterns
4. HANDOUT 75: Four Steps in Making Effective Goals
5. HOMEWORK 53 My Personal Goals

Session Content

1. **Complete Pre-module Quiz**
2. **Review group rules (write rules on board and review verbally—optional)**
3. **Discuss the antecedents for self-medicating and the damages that can occur. Self-medicating can occur when using substances to reduce physical and internal pain. Self-medicating can involve substances or prescribed medication.**
4. **Distribute WORKSHEET 48: Changing My Substance Use Patterns**

   a. Provide nonjudgmental feedback for the reasons for taking this module. The reasons should be tied to the participant's goals.

5. **Provide overview of the program.**

   a. Draw on the board the "You are here" and the "Your goals" circles and describe how the program is designed to fill in the steps to achieve your goals.

Defining a Goal

1. Defining life goals. Write on the board: **"What is a goal?"**

   a. Try to elicit the following response: a goal is something you want to achieve that is important to you—it is personal. You are responsible for achieving your goals. You may need resources and help from others, but you are accountable for whether you reach your goals.

2. Write on the board: **"Why are goals necessary/important?"**

   a. Try to elicit that they help you move in a certain direction, help you achieve what we want out of life, help you be more proud of yourself and can lead to larger goals.

3. Steps in making effective goals. Write on the board: **"What is an effective goal?"** Try to elicit the following three components:

   a. Action: your goal should start with an "action" word.
   b. Achievable: your goal must be realistic for you.
   c. Results: you must be able to see the results and know when you have achieved your goal.

4. **Distribute HANDOUT 75: Four Steps in Making Effective Goals**

    a.   Review the examples with the participants.

5. **Assign HOMEWORK 53: My Personal Goals**

    a.   Inform participants they are to now generate four personal goals that fit the criteria of Action, Achievable, and Results.

Session 2: Assessing Level of Abuse

Objective

This session will:

1. Assess the participant's level of abuse
2. The five levels of use and abuse will be introduced and potential benefits of the program will be emphasized.

The primary objective of this session is to help participants assess their level of substance abuse, and discuss the benefit of this substance abuse module in relation to their goals.

Materials

1. Blackboard or whiteboard (with chalk or markers) or flip chart (with markers)
2. HANDOUT 76: Level of Use
3. HOMEWORK 54: Comparing Level of Use

Session Content

1. **Review HOMEWORK 53: My Personal Goals**

    a.   Be sure to review an example from each group member.

2. **Examine the scores of the Brief Situational Confidence Questionnaire**
3. **Distribute HANDOUT 76: Level of Use**

    a.   Explain that all have different levels and reasons for use and abuse. But there is some common ground that can put us into these five basic categories.
    b.   Emphasize the consequences that use/abuse has had on health and potential legal problems.
    c.   Provide feedback regarding an individual's level of abuse. Feedback should be in small units. It's more important that the participant is encouraged than to point out how wrong they are.

- Although the levels are defined, allow for the participant to have the major input into which category he/she falls into. As the participant progresses in the program, the perception of what level of abuse they are at often changes.

4. Assign HOMEWORK 54: Comparing Level of Use

Session 3: Getting Ready to Change

Objective

This session will:

1. Educate participants on what is needed to make changes
2. Review participants' motivation and stages of change
3. Introduce sources of our behavior (i.e., thoughts/feelings, habits, and environment) as they pertain to substance abuse.

The primary objective of the session is to introduce in neutral terms (examples using non-criminal behavior) those social-cognitive influences that have contributed to our behavior and how we got where we are.

Materials

1. Blackboard or whiteboard (with chalk or markers) or flip chart (with markers)
2. WORKSHEET 49: Personal Change
3. HANDOUT 77 Thoughts, Habits, and Environment Circle of Influence
4. WORKSHEET 50: Case Study—Trish O'Hara
5. HOMEWORK 55: Thoughts, Habits, and Environment

Session Content

1. **Review HOMEWORK 54: Comparing Levels of Use**
2. **Distribute and complete WORKSHEET 49: Personal Change**
3. **Distribute HANDOUT 77: THE Circle of Influence**

   a. A modified version of Bandura's model of behavior is presented
   b. Focus on the first triad

   - Use examples to illustrate how thoughts, habits and environment have led us to where we are in our lives today.
   - Emphasize that these three influences are interrelated and can result in a cycle that prevents you from moving forward.

c.   Now focus on the second triad.

- Reiterate that three areas of our functioning influence us:
  - o   our **Thoughts** and feelings,
  - o   our **Habits** (behavior), and
  - o   our **Environment**.

d.   Be prepared with a POSITIVE example.

- The facilitator should find out information on someone who is well-known (popular) e.g., Taylor Swift. Ask the group what they think that Taylor Swift's Habits are, what her thoughts are about life and music, and how she feels about performing. Where does she spend much of her time and with whom does she likely spend much of her time. What influence do they think her thoughts have on her behavior, or what influence do they think her associates have on her behavior?
  - o   Take time to use at least two situations on how we are influenced by our Thoughts, Habits, and Environment.

4.   **Distribute WORKSHEET 50: Case Study—Trish O'Hara**

a.   Have a group member read the case study aloud and take up the questions during session.

b.   Examine a case study and determine how associates can influence thoughts, habits, and environment.

5.   **Assign HOMEWORK 55: Thoughts, Habits, and Environment**

Session 4: What's It Going to Take to Change?

Objective

This session will:

1.   Introduce a tool (lights) that will assist participants to change the contributors of substance use.

The primary objective of this session is to continue to educate participants about what is needed to make changes in the area of substance abuse.

Materials

1.   Blackboard or whiteboard (with chalk or markers) or flip chart (with markers)
2.   Content Quiz
3.   HANDOUT 78: Strong Motivation
4.   HANDOUT 79: Evaluating Each Area of Thoughts, Habits, and Environment

5. WORKSHEET 51: Using Red and Green Lights
6. HOMEWORK 56: Red, Green, and My Use

Session Content

1. Review HOMEWORK 55: Thoughts, Habits, and Environment
2. Distribute HANDOUT 78: Strong Motivation
3. Distribute HANDOUT 79: Evaluating Each Area of Thoughts, Habits, and Environment

    a. Decisions are important. Presented is a tool to help participants make better decisions.
    b. The focus of this session is to show the participant that they must evaluate the three parts of the Thoughts, Habits, and Environment model.
        • We make decisions on what we think/feel about, what habits we form, and where we go.
    c. In this handout we introduce the stoplight heuristic. It is applied to each area of the Thoughts, Habits, and Environment model.
    d. Red indicates the activity in each area (T-H-E) will directly contribute to substance use.
    e. Yellow means you are not sure but there are indications that not everything they do is on the level (yellow means red is coming).
    f. Green means the area is both not contributing to substance use and is preventing one from substance use.
    g. What is the problem with a neutral relationship or a neutral activity? Neutral (yellow) means red is coming (more on this in Session 7).

4. Distribute WORKSHEET 51: Using Red and Green Lights
5. Assign HOMEWORK 56: Red, Green, and My Use

Session 5: Yellow States (Seemingly Unimportant Thoughts/Feelings, Habits, Environments)

Objective

This session will:

1. Explore the yellow decisions in Thoughts, Habits, and Environment. These thoughts/feelings, habits, and environments move participants closer to use, although they may seem unrelated to substance use.

The primary objective of this session is to help participants continue to evaluate their thoughts/feelings, habits, and environments that put them at risk for substance misuse.

Materials

1. Blackboard or whiteboard (with chalk or markers) or flip chart (with markers)
2. HANDOUT 80: Yellow States
3. HANDOUT 81: Yellow States—Some Examples
4. WORKSHEET 52: Case Study—Peter Fresno
5. WORKSHEET 53: Yellow to Red—Thoughts, Habits, and Environment
6. HOMEWORK 57: Yellow and Green States

Session Content

1. **Review HOMEWORK 56: Red, Green, and My Use**
2. **Distribute HANDOUT 80: Yellow States and HANDOUT 81: Yellow States—Some Examples**

   a. Distinguish between yellow and red states

      • Yellow states may appear to be unrelated to substance use, but upon further examination there is a link to substance use.
      • These seemingly unimportant Thoughts, Habits, and Environment move participants closer to high risk potential for use, although they may seem unrelated to substance use.

   b. Each aspect of Thoughts, Habits, and Environment should be equally emphasized.
   c. How far participants move with his/her yellow states will be based on both the ability to reflect and their stage of change.
   d. Have the group come up with other personal examples.

3. **Distribute WORKSHEET 52: Case Study—Peter Fresno**
4. **Distribute WORKSHEET 53: Yellow to Red—Thoughts, Habits, and Environment**

   a. The purpose of this worksheet is to show how yellow and red states are related.
   b. Have the participant break down the stages of how yellow becomes red in each of the Thoughts, Habits, and Environment areas.
   c. Go over this sufficiently for each participant to understand how their use is related to yellow states. Work through one in a group, then have the participant fill it out individually.
   d. You will likely need several copies of the worksheet for each participant.

5. **Assign HOMEWORK 57: Yellow and Green States**

Session 6: The Chain Leading to Your Use

Objective

This session will:

1. Integrate the three areas of Thoughts, Habits, and Environment into the chain leading to substance use.

The primary objective of this session is to challenge participants on the antecedent thoughts, habits, and environments that lead to substance use.

Materials

1. Blackboard or whiteboard (with chalk or markers) or flip chart (with markers)
2. HANDOUT 82: Leading Up to Substance Use
3. WORKSHEET 54: Your Chain to Substance Use
4. HOMEWORK 58: Final Copy of My Chain

Session Content

1. **Review HOMEWORK 57: Yellow and Green States**
2. **Distribute HANDOUT 82 Leading Up to Substance Use**

   a. Substance use is a behavior that has antecedents and consequences just like any other behavior.

3. **Distribute WORKSHEET 54: Your Chain to Substance Use**

   a. If there are different types of substance use, there may be more than one chain.
   b. The chain begins with an *environment event*, then *thoughts/feelings*, then *behaviors*, then *consequences*. This is a cycle in the chain.

   - Behaviors become habits over time.
   - An event happens, which leads to sad feelings, then a behavior of eating, which in the next cycle of the chain becomes a habit of overeating.
   - Consequences may or may not happen in each cycle within the chain.

     o Some behaviors, at least initially, may not have consequences (i.e., eating)
     o Consequences may or may not include early forms of substance use.

- The final box in the chain will be substance use, in its most severe form.
  - ○ There may be substance use early in the chain, but more cycles will happen before it shows itself in its most severe form.

c. Present an example of the chain board prior to group members completing the worksheets.
d. Have many copies of the worksheet for the participants.
e. These worksheets will be part of the participant's self-management plan.

4. **Assign HOMEWORK 58: Final Copy of My Chain**

Session 7: Refusal Skills

Objective

This session will:

1. Help participants learn and practice skills to avoid substance use (i.e., substance refusal skills).

The primary objective of this session is to teach participants and have participants practice substance use refusal skills.

Materials

1. Blackboard or whiteboard (with chalk or markers) or flip chart (with markers)
2. WORKSHEET 55: Refusal Situations
3. HANDOUT 83: Refusal Bill of Rights
4. WORKSHEET 56: Feedback on Refusal Situations
5. HOMEWORK 59 What I Will Say—Refusal Skills

Session Content

1. **Review HOMEWORK 58: Final Copy of My Chain**
2. **Distribute WORKSHEET 55: Refusal Situations**

a. Have the participants stand-up and face each other. One plays the "provoker" and the other plays the "refuser." Allow for enough time for the "refuser" to react. Do not give feedback at this point in time. The "provoker" should stick to his script.

3. **Distribute HANDOUT 83: Refusal Bill of Rights**

4. **Redo the situations in WORKSHEET 55: Refusal Situations**

   a. Fill out WORKSHEET 56: Feedback on Refusal Situations
   b. Allow the "provoker" more latitude this round
   c. Do at least two ratings per participant
   d. Make may copies of this worksheet
   e. These role-plays should be thoroughly discussed

      • Praise effective demonstration of the skills.

5. **Assign HOMEWORK 59: What I Will Say—Refusal Skills**

Session 8: Changing Environments

Objective

This session will:

1. Assist the participant in changing and participating in environments that are a source of pleasure and have a green light.

The primary objective of this session is to assist the participant in identifying and participating in environments that are a source of pleasure and have a green light.

Materials

1. Blackboard or whiteboard (with chalk or markers) or flip chart (with markers)
2. Content Quiz
3. HANDOUT 84: Activities
4. WORKSHEET 57: Pleasurable Activities (Environment)
5. HOMEWORK 60: A Plan for Changing Environments

Session Content

1. **Distribute HANDOUT 84: Activities**

   a. Environments are one of the earliest points in the substance use chain.
   b. Often people with no plans or scheduled activities are at high risk for substance use.
   c. One of these situations is being at home and alone.

      • Discuss what happens when home alone (list these on the board).

d. The goal is to either create or go to an environment that will be enjoyable or be a source of satisfaction.

- List on wall newsprint the potential activities.

2. **Distribute WORKSHEET 57: Pleasurable Activities (Environment)**

a. Barriers include money, knowing where to look, time, travel, health, skills, and lack of phone, etc.

- Discuss the steps needed to overcome these barriers.

3. **Assign HOMEWORK 60: A Plan for Changing Environments**

Session 9: Changing Habits

Objective

This session will:

1. Introduce skills for changing habits.

The primary objective of this session is to teach participants the skills for changing habits that are related to substance use.

Materials

1. Blackboard or whiteboard (with chalk or markers) or flip chart (with markers)
2. HANDOUT 85: Breaking Down a Habit
3. HANDOUT 86: Steps to Break a Habit
4. WORKSHEET 58: Pick a Yellow Behavior
5. HOMEWORK 61: One Habit

Session Content

1. **Review HOMEWORK 60: A Plan for Changing Environments**
2. **Distribute HANDOUT 85: Breaking Down a Habit**

a. Habits are series of behaviors (routines) that because of our past, we easily do.
b. Habits are not all bad. Habits allow us to do behaviors with little effort.
- A habit, such as showering regularly, can be done without a lot of effort.

c. There are no shortcuts to breaking yellow or red habits
d. A habit involves knowledge, a skill, and desire.

3. **Distribute HANDOUT 86: Steps to Break a Habit**

   a. Brainstorm with the group and list all the "yellow" light routines or behaviors that can lead to substance use
      • Places where suppliers are, overeating, ignoring others, etc.

   b. With the group, list alternate behaviors that can replace the routines or behaviors that lead to a substance use related habit.

4. **Distribute WORKSHEET 58: Pick a Yellow Behavior from Session 7**
5. **Assign HOMEWORK 61: One Habit**

Session 10: Development of the Self-Management Plan

Objective

This session will:

1. Review the module and help the participant create their plan.

The primary objective of this session is to review the content taught and skills developed in this module, and to help participants create a self-management substance use plan.

Materials

1. Post-module Measures
2. WORKSHEET 59: My Self-Management Plan
3. "Substance Abuse" Graduation Certificate
4. Post-module Quiz

Session Content

1. **Review HOMEWORK 61: One Habit**
2. **Distribute WORKSHEET 59: My Self-Management Plan**

   a. Restate your goals
   b. Thoughts/feelings that lead to substance abuse and skills that will assist
   c. Habits that lead to substance abuse and skills that will assist
   d. Environment factors that lead to substance abuse and skills that will assist.

3. **Distribute "Substance Abuse" Graduation Certificate**
4. **Post-module Quiz**

References

American Psychiatric Association. (2013). *DSM-5 Self-Rated Level 1 Cross-Cutting Symptom Measure-Adult*. Retrieved from www.psychiatry.org/.../Practice/DSM/APA_DSM5_Level-1-Measure-Adult.pdf

Andrews, D. A., & Bonta, J. (2010). *The psychology of criminal conduct* (5th ed.). New Providence, NJ: LexisNexis Matthew Bender.

Beck, A. T. (1964). Thinking and depression: II. Theory and therapy. *Archives of General Psychiatry, 10*, 561–571.

Beck, A. T. (1970). The core problem in depression: The cognitive triad. In J. Masserman (Ed.), *Depression: Theories and therapies*. New York: Grune & Stratton.

Beck, J. S. (1995). *Cognitive therapy: Basics and beyond*. New York: Guilford Press.

Breslin, F. C., Sobell, L. C., Sobell, M. B., & Agrawal, S. (1999). Brief situational confidence questionnaire. *Psyctests*. https://doi.org/10.1037/t11336-000

Bush, J. M., & Bilodeau, B. (1993). *Options: A cognitive change program*. Washington, DC: National Institute of Corrections.

Connors, G. J., Walitzer, K. S., & Dermen, K. H. (2002). Preparing clients for alcoholism treatment: Effects on treatment participation and outcomes. *Journal of Consulting and Clinical Psychology, 70*, 1161–1169.

Corrigan, P. W. (2003). Towards an integrated structural model of psychiatric rehabilitation. *Psychiatric Rehabilitation Journal, 26*, 346–357. doi: 10.2975/26.2003.346.354

Corrigan, P. W., Mueser, K. T., Bond, G. R., Drake, R. E., & Solomon, P. (2008). Peer services and supports. In *Principles and practice of psychiatric rehabilitation: An empirical approach* (pp. 359–378). New York: Guilford Press.

Day, A., Howells, K., Casey, S., Ward, T., Chambers, J. C., & Birgden, A. (2009). Assessing treatment readiness in violent offenders. *Journal of Interpersonal Violence, 24*(4), 618–635. https://doi.org/10.1177/0886260508317200

Drake, R. E., Wallach, M. A., & McGovern, M. P. (2005). Special section on relapse prevention: Future directions in preventing relapse to substance abuse among clients with severe mental illness. *Psychiatric Services, 56*, 1297–1302.

D'zurilla, T. J., & Goldfried, M. R. (1971). Problem solving and behavior modification. *Journal of Abnormal Psychology, 78*(1), 107.

Gendreau, P. (1996). The principles of effective intervention with offenders. In A. T. Garland (Ed.), *Choosing correctional options that work: Defining the demand and evaluating the supply* (pp. 117–130). Thousand Oaks, CA: Sage.

Giffort, D., Schmook, A., Woody, C., Vollendorf, C., & Gervain, M. (1995). *Recovery assessment scale*. Chicago: Illinois Department of Mental Health.

Howells, K., & Day, A. (2007). Readiness for treatment in high risk offenders with personality disorders. *Psychology, Crime, & Law*, *13*, 47–56.

Kroner, D. G., & Takahashi, M. (2012). Every session counts: The differential impact of previous programmes and current programme dosage on offender recidivism. *Legal and Criminological Psychology*, *17*(1), 136–150. https://doi.org/10.1111/j.2044-8333.2010.02001.x

McGuire, J. (2003). Maintaining change: Converging legal and psychological initiatives in a therapeutic jurisprudence framework. *Western Criminology Review*, *4*, 108–123.

McNiel, D., Eisner, J. P., & Binder, R. L. (2003). The relationship between aggressive attributional style and violence. *Journal of Consulting and Clinical Psychology*, *71*, 399–403.

Miller, W. R., & Rollnick, S. (1999). *Motivational interviewing: Preparing people for change*. New York: Guilford Press.

Miller, W. R., & Tonigan, J. S. (1996). Assessing drinkers' motivation for change: The Stages of Change Readiness and Treatment Eagerness Scale (SOCRATES). *Psychology of Addictive Behaviors*, *10*, 81–89.

Mills, J. F., Kroner, D. G., & Forth, A. E. (2002). Measures of Criminal Attitudes and Associates (MCAA) development, factor structure, reliability, and validity. *Assessment*, *9*(3), 240–253.

Monahan, J., & Steadman, H. J. (2001). Violence risk assessment: A quarter century of research. In L. E. Frost & R. J. Bonnie (Eds.), *The evolution of mental health law*. Washington, DC: American Psychological Association.

Morgan, R.D., & Flora, D.B. (2002). Group psychotherapy with incarcerated offenders: A research synthesis. *Group Dynamics: Theory, Research, and Practice*, *6*, 203–218. doi:10.1037//1089-2699.6.3.203

Morgan, R. D., Kroner, D. G., Mills, J. F., Bauer, R., & Serna, C. (2014). Treating justice involved persons with mental illness: Preliminary evaluation of a comprehensive treatment program. *Criminal Justice and Behavior*, *41*, 902–916.

Morgan, R. D., Van Horn, S. A., & Hunter, J. T. (2017). Changing lives and changing outcomes: Community outcomes from an intervention for justice-involved persons with mental illness. Manuscript in preparation for publication.

Novaco, R. W. (1994). Anger as a risk factor for violence among the mentally disordered. In J. Monahan & H. J. Steadman (Eds.), *Violence and mental disorder: Developments in risk assessment*. Chicago: University of Chicago Press.

Prochaska, J. O., DiClemente, C. C., & Norcross, J. C. (1992). In search of how people change: Applications to addictive behaviors. *American Psychologist*, *47*, 1102–1114.

Skeem, J. L., Schubert, C., Odgers, C., Mulvey, E. P., Gardner, W., & Lidz, C. (2006). Psychiatric symptoms and community violence among high-risk patients: A test of the relationship at the weekly level. *Journal of Consulting and Clinical Psychology*, *74*, 967–979.

Thompson, K., Kulkarni, J., & Sergejew, A. A. (2000). Reliability and validity of a new Medication Adherence Rating Scale (MARS) for the psychoses. *Schizophrenia Research*, *42*(3), 241–247.

Van Horn, S. A., Morgan, R. D., Brusman-Lovins, L., Littlefield, A., Hunter, J. T., & Gigax, G. (2017). *Changing lives, changing outcomes: "What works" in an intervention for justice-involved persons with mental illness*. Manuscript submitted for publication.

Walters, G. D. (1990). *The criminal lifestyle: Patterns of serious criminal conduct*. Thousand Oaks, CA: Sage.

Walters, G. D. (2006). *The Psychological Inventory of Criminal Thinking Styles (PICTS) professional manual*. Allentown, PA: Center for Lifestyle Studies.

Watson, D., Clark, L. A., & Tellegen, A. (1988). Development and validation of brief measures of positive and negative affect: The PANAS scales. *Journal of Personality and Social Psychology, 54*(6), 1063.

Williams, E. C., Kivlahan, D. R., Saitz, R., Merrill, J. O., Achtmeyer, C. E., McCormick, K. A., & Bradley, K. A. (2006). Readiness to change in primary care patients who screened positive for alcohol misuse. *Annals of Family Medicine, 4*, 213–220.

Yalom, I. D., & Leszcz, M. (2005). *Theory and practice of group psychotherapy*. New York: Basic Books.

Yochelson, S., & Samenow, S. E. (1976). *The criminal personality: Volume I. A profile for change*. Northvale, NJ: Jason Aronson.

Yochelson, S., & Samenow, S. E. (1977). *The criminal personality: Volume II. The change process*. Northvale, NJ: Jason Aronson.

Index

Note: Page numbers in bold indicate a table on the corresponding page.